Parliamentary Procedure Handbook

The Ultimate Guide for Learning Parliamentary Procedure and Effective Meeting Skills

A practical book written by a teacher with 32 years of experience teaching parliamentary procedure and meeting management skills

Christopher G. Yorke, M. Ed

Parliamentary Procedure Handbook

By Christopher G. Yorke, M. Ed.

Published by:

Mason Creek Publishing
1238 24th Ave.
Longview, WA 98632
(360)600-9615
cyorke57@gmail.com

ISBN 978-1793960221
Printed in the United States of America
Library of Congress CIP Data pending

Table of Contents

Preface

The Parliamentary Procedure Handbook was written for all of those individuals who would like to learn parliamentary procedure and effective meeting skills. Whether you want to actually manage meetings as a chairperson or participate effectively as a member in a meeting, this book will help you learn what you need to be successful.

There are hundreds of references on the market dealing with parliamentary procedure, but most of them are confusing and hard to understand. This book will help you master the main principles of parliamentary procedure and become an effective participant in your organization.

The best way to really learn Parliamentary Procedure is to use it. After reading the handbook and completing the exercises, be sure to bring it with you to your next meeting. You can refer to the motions charts as needed during your meeting.

Think of parliamentary procedure as a game - have fun with it! Your influence in meetings and other gatherings will soon be obvious.

Christopher G. Yorke

CHAPTER 1
Introduction to Parliamentary Procedure

What is Parliamentary Procedure?

Parliamentary Procedure is used by many organizations, including businesses, government agencies, leadership clubs, school boards, fair boards, and community groups to help run organized and productive business meetings. The procedures used are merely a set of rules based on parliamentary law. Parliamentary Procedure is a democratic method of conducting business because it assures that all sides of an issue are treated fairly, and that everyone is given an opportunity to voice an opinion and to vote.

Parliamentary Procedure is useful to everyone. Knowing how to use the basic skills of Parliamentary Procedure will help you to express your ideas and opinions in meetings and other group functions. It will also help you to develop confidence in your speaking ability. Have you ever sat in a meeting knowing that you had ideas you wished to share, but could not because you were unsure of how to bring your ideas forward to the group? Parliamentary Procedure will help you to develop your oral communication abilities, and help you to explain your ideas. Being able to communicate effectively in meetings and group situations is an essential leadership skill.

Parliamentary Procedure
Key Terms You Should Know

ASSEMBLY

The group of members at a meeting.

BUSINESS AT HAND

The current business being dealt with in a meeting.

CHAIR, CHAIRPERSON

The person in charge of conducting the meeting.

CONSIDERATION

To discuss and decide on an item of business in a meeting.

COMMIT

To refer a motion to a committee.

COMMITTEE

A small group of people within an organization who have a specific task or project to complete.

DELEGATE

To give someone a task or job to be completed.

FLOOR

To have the "floor" is to have been recognized by the chairperson and have the right to speak before the assembly.

GERMANE

To be relevant and to relate to the pending motion or to the business at hand.

MAKER OF THE MOTION

A person who makes a motion during a meeting.

MOTION

A motion is a formal way for a member to bring an idea or item of business before the assembly. It is accomplished in the form of a "main motion."

NOMINATIONS
The candidates who are selected by the members to run for officer or other positions within an organization.

PENDING
The current motion or business before the assembly.

PRESIDING OFFICER
The officer in charge of a meeting. Normally the president.

PREVAILING
To be on the winning side of a vote.

QUESTION
When a motion has been made and seconded the chair makes a formal statement of the motion to the assembly by stating the "question." Another way of saying "the vote," as in "Are you ready for the question? " "Are you ready to vote?"

RATIFY
To give formal approval for some action or procedure.

SECOND
To announce "second" once a motion is made in a meeting, is to indicate that you also support bringing the motion before the assembly for discussion. Many motions must receive a second in order to be discussed, or they die.

SUSTAIN
To agree with and thereby support a decision made by the chairperson.

RECOGNIZED
To be given the right to speak by the chairperson. You must be Recognized before you can speak, except in certain situations. To be recognized you should stand and address the chair as follows; "Mr. President," or "Madam President".

YIELD THE FLOOR
When a member finishes speaking, he or she "yields the floor," or gives the floor back to the chairperson, by resuming his or her seat.

CHAPTER ONE
KEY TERMS YOU SHOULD KNOW

Matching Review

- **Match each term with its definition from page 5**

1. Assembly _____

2. Business at hand _____

3. Chairperson _____

4. Consideration _____

5. Commit _____

6. Committee _____

7. Delegate _____

8. Floor _____

9. Germane _____

10. Motion _____

11. Nominations _____

12. Pending _____

13. Presiding officer _____

14. Prevailing _____

15. Question _____

16. Ratify _____

17. Second _____

18. Sustain _____

19. Recognized _____

20. Yield the floor _____

Matching Review Answer Choices

a. To agree with the chair

b. Person in charge at a meeting

c. Small group with a specific job

d. To be relevant to the motion

e. To be on the winning side

f. To finish speaking and sit down

g. Do this before you speak

h. Must happen before a motion can be discussed

i. Normally the president

j. Refer to a committee

k. Current motion before the group

l. All the members

m. To be recognized and have the right to speak

n. Formal approval

o. To discuss an item or motion

p. Formal statement of a motion by the chair

q. Select candidates to run for office

r. The current business

s. Give someone a task

t. A formal way for a member to bring an idea or item of business be
    fore the assembly

CHAPTER ONE
INTRODUCTION TO
PARLIAMENTARY PROCEDURE

Crossword One

Clues on page 7

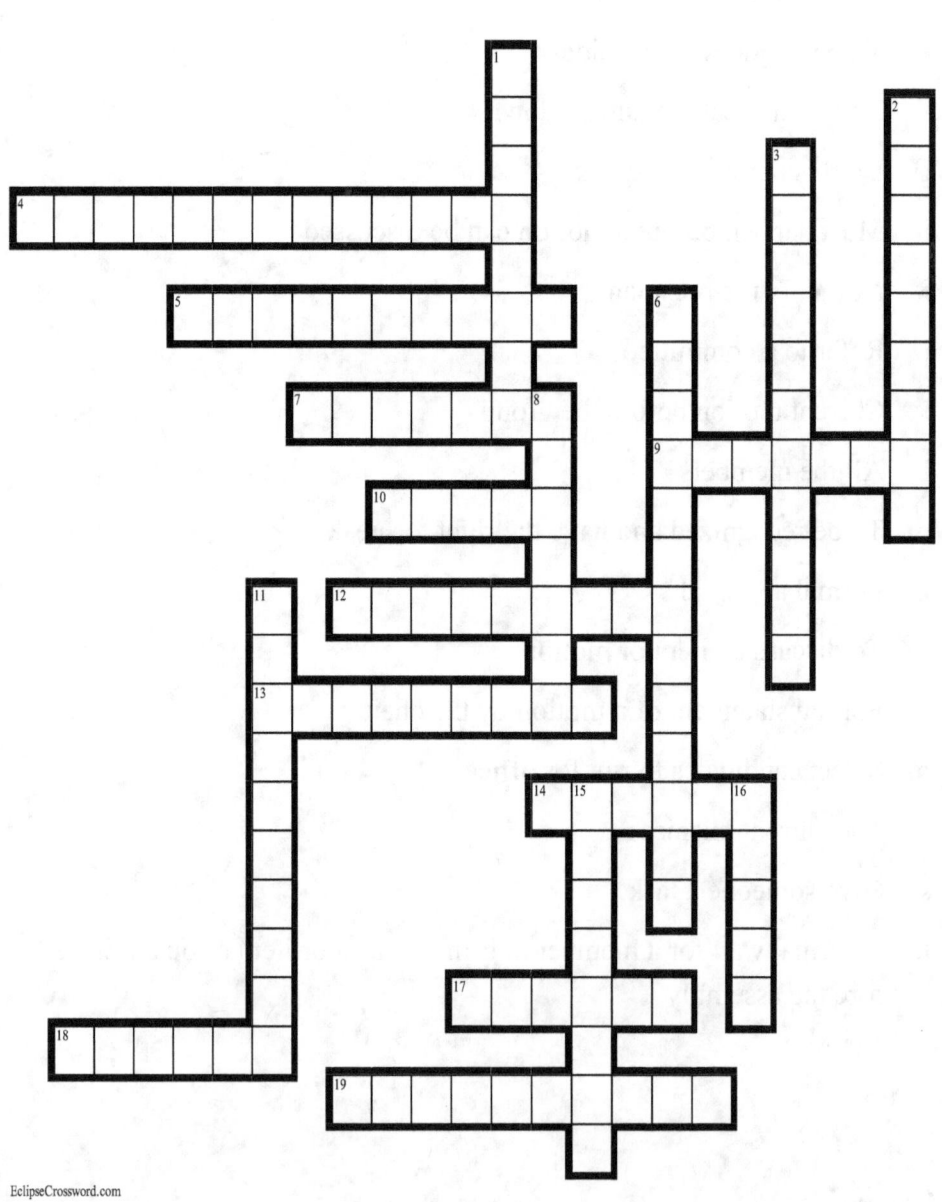

CHAPTER ONE
INTRODUCTION TO
PARLIAMENTARY PROCEDURE
Crossword One Clues

Across

4. Parli pro is used by many _____.

5. Parli pro is a _____ method of conducting business.

7. Current motion.

9. Agree with the decision of the chair.

10. To be recognized and have the right to speak.

12. Give someone a task to complete.

13. Small group given a specific task.

14. Give formal approval.

17. To refer a motion to a committee.

18. Many motions must receive this before discussion.

19. Winning side of a vote.

Down

1. The vote.

2. Officer in charge of a meeting.

3. Selected by the members to run for office.

6. To discuss at a meeting.

8. Relevant to the pending motion.

11. Must do this before you can speak.

15. The group at a meeting.

16. Give the floor back to the chairperson.

CHAPTER ONE
INTRODUCTION TO
PARLIAMENTARY PROCEDURE

True/False Review Quiz One

1. Parliamentary Procedure is used by many organizations including businesses and schools.

2. Parliamentary Procedure is a set of rules for conducting meetings.

3. Parliamentary Procedure is a democratic method of conducting business because it assures that only officers or managers get to speak.

4. Knowing how to use the basic skills of Parliamentary Procedure will help you to express your ideas and opinions in meetings and other group functions.

5. Being able to communicate effectively in meetings and group situations is an essential leadership skill.

6. The business planned for a future meeting is called the business at hand.

7. The chairperson, or chair, is responsible for organizing all of the chairs for a group meeting.

8. To discuss and decide on an item of business in a meeting is called giving the item consideration.

9. A committee normally consists of a large group of people given a task.

10. To have the "floor" is to have been recognized by the chairperson and have the right to speak before the assembly.

11. A person who makes a motion during a meeting is called the mover of the motion.

12. The current motion or business before the assembly is called pending.

13. To be on the losing side of a vote is to be on the prevailing side.

14. A motion is a formal way for a member to bring an idea or item of business before the assembly.

15. When a motion has been made and seconded the chair places it before the assembly by stating the "question."

16. Many motions must receive a second in order to be discussed or they die.

17. Something that is germane does not relate to the pending business.

18. The pending business is not the business at hand.

19. To be recognized in a meeting is to be given the right to speak by the chairperson.

20. When a member finishes speaking, he or she "yields the floor."

The Four Objectives of
Parliamentary Procedure

1. Only one subject may be dealt with at a time.

The chairman should make sure members of the meeting complete an item of business before moving on to something else. Each item should be discussed and voted upon.

2. Extend courtesy to everyone.

Each person in the meeting should be treated respectfully and should be given an equal opportunity to speak and present ideas.

3. Observe the rule of the majority

When items of business are voted on, the resulting decision will be based on the will of the majority. This will mean a **majority vote** or a **two-thirds vote**, depending on the motion **on the floor**.

4. Ensure the rights of the minority.

Even those with opinions different from that of the majority shall have an equal opportunity to express their ideas. It is fine if members disagree as long as they avoid personal attacks on one another.

Order of Business

The "order of business" is the order in which business should be dealt with in a meeting. An order of business will help members stay on track and assist them in taking care of business as it needs to be conducted. The following order of business is an example used in some organizations.

Opening ceremony

Reading and approval of the minutes from the previous meeting

Reports of Officers, Boards, and Standing Committees

Reports of Special Committees

Unfinished business (from previous meetings)

New Business
Closing ceremony

Optional Items after new business:

Items for the good of the order

Announcements

Program - films, guest speakers, etc.

Refreshments

Agenda

An agenda is an order of business adopted for a specific meeting or session. It includes specific items of business that need to be dealt with during the meeting. An agenda sets expectations for a meeting and helps keep everyone at the meeting on track so time is not wasted. Some pointers for utilizing a meeting agenda are listed below.

- The group leader should request input for the agenda from group members at least two weeks prior to the meeting.

- Topics for the agenda should be important to the team and organization.

- Include the names of members who will be responsible for leading the discussion on each topic.

- Include a heading for the agenda with the name of the group/team, date, time, and location of the meeting.

- List items in the agenda using the "order of business" format on page 11.

- Send the agenda out to interested parties at least one week prior to the meeting. This allows people time to prepare for the meeting.

- See the example agenda on page 13.

Example Agenda

Marketing Team Meeting
Time: 7:00 p.m.
Date: March 12, 2018
Location: Meeting room at XYZ, Inc.

Opening ceremony (if required) - Bill (President or whomever is chairing the meeting)

Minutes of the previous meeting - Mary (Secretary)

Reports of Officers, Boards, and Standing Committees

Staff recreation committee report - Stan and Jane

Budget report - Joanna (Treasurer)

Reports of Special Committees

Building air conditioning repair - Larry

Unfinished business (from previous meetings)

Decide on location of new marketing display as proposed at last meeting - Sue

New Business

Upcoming marketing conference - who should attend?
How to launch new XYZ product?

Items for the good of the order

Anything members would like to bring up.

Announcements

Remember to register for the spring marketing conference

Program - films, guest speakers.

Closing Ceremonies - Bill

Minutes

The official record of the proceedings of a meeting is called the minutes. Minutes are recorded by the secretary and kept on file. Minutes should contain what was done at a meeting, not what each member said.

Content of the minutes

First Paragraph
The type of meeting -- regular, special, etc.

Name of the organization.

Date, time, and location of the meeting.

Presiding officer's and secretary's name.

The number of members present. For small groups it is customary to record the name of each member present.

Approval of the minutes from the previous meeting.

Correct Procedure for Approval of the Minutes

Before a meeting begins the minutes of the previous meeting need to be read by the secretary and approved by the members. This is called "Approval of the Minutes." (See the following example)

Chair: *"The Secretary will read the minutes of the January 14, 2018 meeting."*

Secretary: Stands and reads the minutes.

Chair: *"Are there any corrections to the minutes?"* (Pause)

Chair: *"If there are no corrections, the minutes stand approved as read." or "If there are no further corrections, the minutes stand approved as corrected."*

Body of the Minutes

The body of the minutes should contain a separate paragraph for each subject dealt with in the meeting.

Each paragraph should contain the following information:

- The item of business or topic being addressed.
- Each significant motion proposed.
- Include main motions or motions that bring a question again before the group, primary and secondary amendments, and secondary motions adhering to the main motion. *(Do not need to record withdrawn motions in most cases).*
- The name of the person making each motion.
- Whether or not the motion was discussed can be mentioned briefly.
- Record the resulting vote --- pass or fail. For standing votes record the number for and the number against the motion.
- All notices of motions to be dealt with at upcoming meetings.
- All points of order or appeals, whether they were sustained or lost (passed or failed), and the reasons for the chair's ruling.

Last Paragraph
1. The hour of adjournment.

The secretary should sign the minutes.

Respectfully submitted, (optional)
Secretary's Signature

See the example minutes on page 16.

XYZ Marketing Department Meeting

March 12, 2018

Minutes

The March 12, 2018 meeting of the XYZ Marketing Team Meeting was called to order at 7:00 p.m. by Bill Taft, Chairperson. The meeting was held in the Conference room at XYZ, Inc. Twenty members were present.

MINUTES OF THE PREVIOUS MEETING
The minutes of the January 14, 2018 meeting were read and approved as read.

REPORTS OF OFFICERS, BOARDS, AND STANDING COMMITTEES
Nicole Wong, Treasurer, reported that there is $82,000 in the marketing dept. treasury. Bill Taft gave a report on the progress of the new XYZ product. Stacy Heart, Chairperson of the staff recreation committee, reported that the spring volleyball tournament will be held at Lewisville Park on April 21, 2018.

UNFINISHED BUSINESS
Kristin Weber announced that the motion made at the January 14, 2018 meeting by Andy Jones, that the department send four members to the National Marketing Convention, postponed until this meeting, was now on the floor for further discussion. After considerable debate the motion passed.

NEW BUSINESS
Art Wilson moved that the department hold an auction sometime in the summer of 2018 in order to raise money to pay for new furniture for the break room Discussion followed. John Smith moved to refer the motion to a committee of three, appointed by the chair, to research the idea and report back at the May meeting. Motion passed. The committee is: Frank Clark, Danielle Mason, and Mary Garner, (chair).

PROGRAM

Corrine Simon and Heather Lewis gave a video presentation on their trip to the Washington D.C. Conference.

Crystal Paulus moved to adjourn the meeting. Motion passed. The meeting was adjourned at 8:00 p.m.

Refreshments followed the meeting.

Respectfully Submitted,

Kristin Weber, Secretary

Reading and Approval of the Minutes

The minutes of the previous meeting should be read and approved immediately after the opening of the current meeting.

Chair:
"The Secretary will read the minutes."

The Secretary stands and reads the minutes from the previous meeting.

Chair:
"Are there any corrections to the minutes?"

(pause)

If there are no corrections.

Chair:
"If there are no corrections the minutes stand approved as read."

If there are any corrections brought forth by the members they are usually handled by general (unanimous) consent.

Member:
States corrections to the minutes.

Chair:
"If there is no objection the minutes stand approved as corrected."

CHAPTER ONE
THE FOUR OBJECTIVES, ORDER OF BUSINESS, AGENDA, MINUTES

Fill in the Blank Review

1. Only one _____ may be dealt with at a time.

2. Each item of business should be discussed and _____ upon.

3. Each person in a meeting should be given an _____ opportunity to speak and present ideas.

4. In a meeting we should observe the rule of the _____.

5. In meetings we should make sure to ensure the rights of the _____.

6. The "order of business" is the order in which _____ should be dealt with in a meeting.

7. An _____ is an order of business adopted for a specific meeting or session.

8. The group leader should request _____ for the agenda from group members.

9. Before a meeting begins the minutes should be read by the secretary and _____ by the members.

10. The minutes are normally recorded by the _____.

CHAPTER ONE
THE FOUR OBJECTIVES, ORDER OF BUSINESS, AGENDA, MINUTES

Crossword Two

Clues on page 21

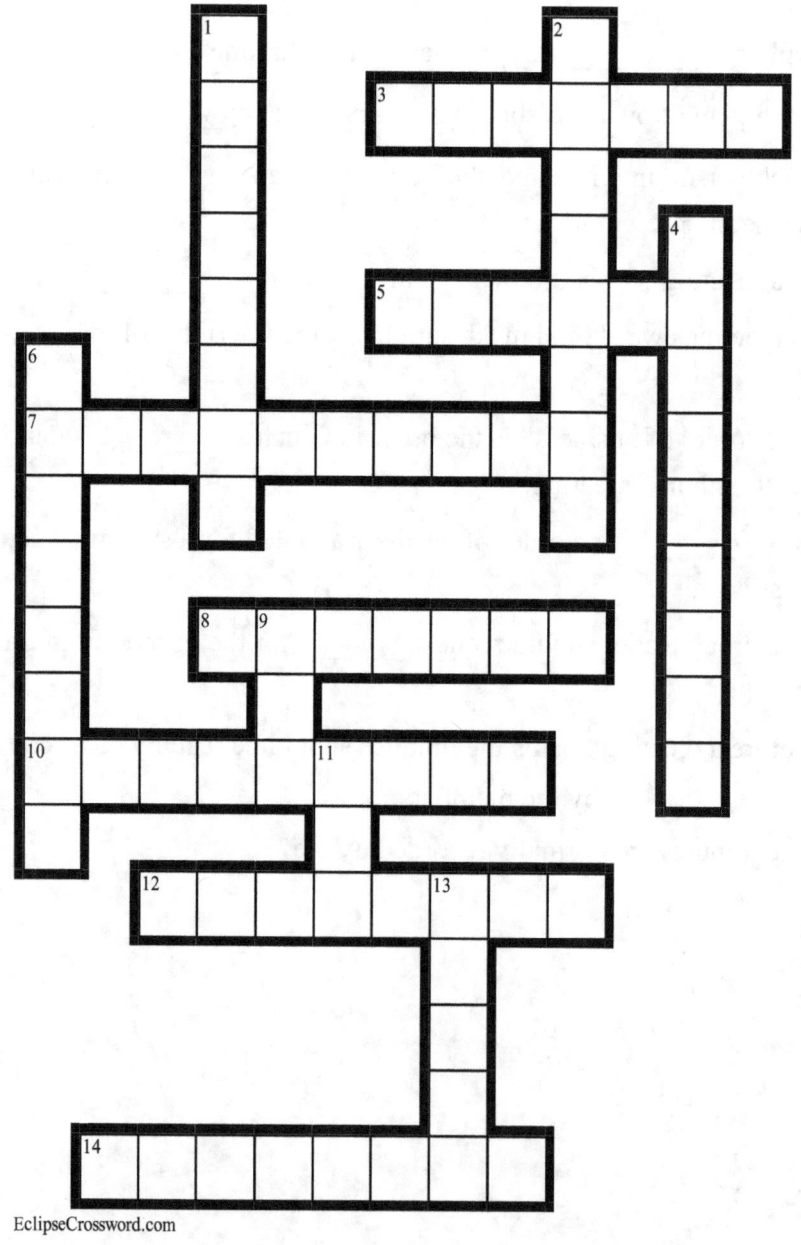

CHAPTER ONE
THE FOUR OBJECTIVES, ORDER OF BUSINESS, AGENDA, MINUTES

Crossword Two Clues

Across

3. Official record of the proceedings at a meeting.

5. Adopted for a specific meeting.

7. Parliamentary procedure has four of these.

8. The body of the minutes should contain these.

10. Reads the minutes of the previous meeting to the group.

12. Ensure the rights of this.

14. Observe the rule of this.

Down

1. Minutes of the previous meeting must be _____ .

2. The order of.

4. The body of the minutes should contain a separate _____ for each subject dealt with in the meeting.

6. Should be extended to everyone in a meeting.

9. The number of subjects that can be dealt with at a time.

11. Number of gavel taps to start a meeting.

13. The group leader should request this when making a meeting agenda.

CHAPTER ONE
THE FOUR OBJECTIVES, ORDER OF BUSINESS, AGENDA, MINUTES

True/False Review Quiz Two

1. With parliamentary procedure up to 3 subjects can be dealt with at a time.

2. Observing the rule of the majority means that each person should be given the opportunity to speak.

3. Courtesy should be extended to everyone during a meeting.

4. Members in a meeting are not allowed to disagree.

5. The will of the majority is determined by those members that speak the loudest.

6. The will of the majority is determined by a majority or a two-thirds vote.

7. The order in which business should be dealt with in a meeting is called the agenda.

8. The agenda and the order of business are actually the same thing.

9. An agenda includes specific items of business that need to be dealt with in a meeting.

10. The group leader should determine items to put on an agenda.

11. The agenda for a meeting should be sent out to all interested parties at least one day prior to the meeting.

12. The "Minutes" refers to the time length of a meeting.

13. The official record of the proceedings at a meeting is call the "Minutes."

14. The "Minutes" should include a separate paragraph for each subject dealt with in a meeting.

The Gavel

The president or chairperson normally conducts a business meeting. It is the presiding officer's responsibility to keep the meeting flowing in an orderly manner and to make sure that the business is conducted in a fair and organized fashion. The chairperson uses a gavel for two main purposes, to keep the meeting on track and to signal the passage or failure of any motions that are brought by the group. A motion is simply a formal way for a member to present an idea for the group to discuss and vote on.

Proper Use of the Gavel

One Tap
Tells members to be seated.   Chair: *"Please be seated."*
To pass or fail a motion.   Chair: *"The motion passes."* or
                                                "The motion fails."
To adjourn the meeting.   Chair: *"The meeting is adjourned."*

Two Taps
To start a meeting.   Chair: *"The meeting will come to
                                                order."*

Three Taps
Signal for all members to stand.   Chair: *"Please rise."*
Stand for opening ceremonies.   Chair: *"Please rise."*
Stand for salute to the Flag.   Chair: *"Please rise."*

Series of Sharp Taps
To bring order to a meeting that has become unruly.
Chair: *"Please come to order."*

Voting Procedures

Common Methods of Voting

Voice Vote

By saying "aye" (in favor) or "no." This is the customary method of voting on a motion.

Rising Vote

A *Rising Vote* is called for when the presiding officer, or a member, has doubts about a previous vote. Those in favor of a motion are called upon to stand and a count is taken. Then those opposed to a proposition are called upon to stand and a count is taken. Also, a rising vote is used to verify an inconclusive voice vote, and in motions requiring a two-thirds vote for its adoption.

Secret Ballot

A secret ballot is a written vote, it is used to maintain the secrecy of each member's vote.

Roll Call

In a roll call vote the secretary polls the group and records how each member votes.

Hand Vote

A hand vote, where members simply raise there hands, can be used in place of a rising vote in small meetings or assemblies. A hand vote can also be used in place of a voice vote if desired by the membership.

Majority

A majority vote requires that more than half of the members present must vote in favor of a motion for it to pass. For example, if 100 members were present 51 would have to vote in favor to pass a motion. If there is a tie, the president's vote may be used to break it. Also, the president may vote to make a tie. In this case the motion would fail because a majority would not be obtained.

Two-Thirds Vote

A two-thirds vote requires that two-thirds of the members must vote in favor of a motion for it to pass. A two-thirds vote is needed when a motion will limit the rights of a member or members of the organization. In a meeting with 60 members present, 40 would have to vote in favor in order to pass a motion. A rising vote is used to verify a two-thirds vote.

Plurality Vote

A plurality vote is the largest number of votes to be given to a candidate or proposition when there are three or more choices possible. Whichever candidate or proposition receives the largest number of vote has a plurality. For example, if there are three candidates running for office and one receives 10 votes, another receives 8 votes, and another receives 6 votes, the first candidate would have a plurality. Note that 10 votes in this case would not be a majority.

Quorum

A quorum is the number of vote-entitled members who must be present at a meeting in order for business to be legally transacted. A quorum can be set at any number by the organization. If no quorum is set, it is automatically set at half of the members plus one, which would be a majority.

CHAPTER ONE
GAVEL, VOTING PROCEDURES

Review Questions

1. What are the two main purposes of using a gavel?

    Write down the correct number of gavel taps for items 2 through 8.

2. Start a meeting.

3. Pass or fail a motion.

4. Bring order to an unruly meeting.

5. Ask members to stand.

6. Adjourn a meeting.

7. Ask members to be seated.

8. What is the customary method of voting?

9. List two reasons a chairperson might call for a rising vote.

10. What kind of vote is it where the secretary polls the members of the group?

11. Which type of vote can be used instead of a rising vote?

12. If there were 30 members at a meeting, how many would have to vote in favor of a motion for it to pass when a majority vote is required?

13. What kind of vote is required when a motion will limit or reduce the rights of the members?

14. Three candidates were nominated to run for President of a club. Candidate one received 12 votes, candidate two received 18 votes, and candidate three received 7 votes. Which candidate received a plurality?

15. How many members would make a quorum in a meeting of 50 members where there is a 20% quorum?

CHAPTER ONE
GAVEL, VOTING PROCEDURES

Crossword Three
Clues on page 28

CHAPTER ONE
GAVEL, VOTING PROCEDURES

Crossword Three Clues

Across

4. Three taps of the gavel to ask members to do this.

5. One tap of the gavel is used to pass or fail this.

6. The largest number of votes to be given a candidate when there are three or more choices.

8. The number of gavel taps to request all members to stand.

11. One tap of the gavel at the end of a meeting.

13. Vote against.

14. A written vote.

15. Can be used for rising vote.

Down

1. The number of vote entitled members who must be present.

2. Chairperson uses this tool to keep meetings on track.

3. Role call vote.

7. In favor.

8. The number of gavel taps to start a meeting.

9. Customary method of voting on a motion.

10. A vote of more than half the members.

12. Vote by standing.

True/False Quiz Three

1. A gavel helps the chairperson keep a meeting on track.

2. Three taps of the gavel signals the members that the meeting will begin.

3. One tap of the gavel signals that a motion has passed.

4. Three taps of the gavel signals that a motion has failed.

5. The voice vote is the customary method of voting on a motion.

6. With a voice vote members say "yes" or "no."

7. A majority vote requires two-thirds for adoption.

8. A secret ballot is also known as a rising vote.

9. With a hand vote members clap their hands.

10. Fifty one out of one hundred members would be a majority.

11. Forty five out of ninety members would be needed for a two-thirds vote to pass.

12. A rising vote is used to verify a two-thirds vote.

13. A plurality vote is the largest number of votes to be given to a candidate or proposition when there are three or more choices possible.

14. A quorum is the number of vote-entitled members who must be present in order for business to be legally transacted.

15. A quorum must be set at 10% of the membership.

CHAPTER TWO
Motions

There are many different motions used in parliamentary procedure. *A motion is simply a formal way of saying what you want to happen in a meeting.* Using correct motions will give you the ability to bring forth your ideas and opinions for consideration by the group. All of the motions are listed below by class. There are five groups or classes of motions. The page number where each motion can be found is shown in the table of contents.

Classes of Motions

1. **Main Motions**

   A main motion is a motion that brings business before the group. Main motions are made while no other motion is pending.
   Main Motion
   Incidental Main Motions - Adopt, Ratify

2. **Subsidiary Motions**

   A subsidiary motion is a type of motion by which a group deals directly with a main motion prior to, or instead of, voting on the main motion itself.
   Postpone Indefinitely
   Amend
   Refer to a Committee
   Postpone Definitely
   Limit or Extend Limits of Debate
   Previous Question
   Lay on the Table

3. Privileged Motions

Motions which do not relate to the pending question (motion) but have to do with matters of such urgency or importance that, without discussion (debate), are allowed to interrupt the consideration of anything else.

Call for the Orders of the Day

Question of Privilege

Recess

Adjourn

Fix the Time to Which to Adjourn

4. Incidental Motions

An incidental motion is a motion that relates to the main motion and other parliamentary motions. They take precedence over any pending question (motion) out of which they arise. This means they must be dealt with first; they have priority over other motions on the floor.

Point of Order

Appeal

Suspend the Rules

Objection to the Consideration of a Question

Division of a Question

Division of the Assembly (House)

Parliamentary Inquiry

Point of Information

Withdraw a Motion

5. Motions that bring a question again before the assembly

These motions bring a question (motion) back for further considera-tion by the group. They can be discussed and voted on as necessary.

Take From the Table

Rescind

Reconsider

Main Motion

The main motion is used by any individual at a meeting to bring forward an item of business, an idea, or a proposal for adoption by the group.

Details:

- **The maker of this motion must first be recognized by the chair.**
- **The motion is out of order when another person has the floor.**
- **Requires a second.**
- **Debatable (the motion can be discussed).**
- **Amendable (the motion can be modified).**
- **Majority vote (one more than half of the members in favor).**
- **Can be reconsidered (can a bring a motion back up to the group).**

How a Main Motion Should Progress

A member rises and addresses the presiding officer or chairperson.
> Proper way to address the chair:
> Mr. Chairperson or Mr. President
> Madam Chairperson or Madam President
> Mr./Madam Chairman can be used if people prefer. There is a lot of debate about whether or not "Chairman" is appropriate these days. It is up to the preference of the person leading the meeting.

The member is recognized by the chair.

The member proposes a motion.

Another member seconds the motion.

The presiding officer states the motion or <u>question</u> to the assembly/group and calls for discussion.

The members discuss or debate the motion. The maker of the motion has the first right to discuss the motion.

The presiding officer takes a voice vote on the motion.

The presiding officer announces the result of the vote and the effect of the motion.

Question

The "question" refers to the formal statement by the chair of the motion presented by a member of the group. As in, "are you ready for the question."

Examples

Chair: *"It has been moved and seconded to host an awards banquet. Are you ready for the question."*

Or less formally: *"Is there any discussion." or "What is the pleasure of the group."*

Main Motion Example

The main motion is used to bring an item of business, an idea, or a proposal before the group. The correct way to propose a motion is to say, *"I move that..."* or *"I move to..."* Never say, *"I motion that..."*

Member:
"Madam Chairperson."

Chair:
"The chair recognizes John." or just *"John."*

Member:
"I move that the department host an awards banquet at the end of the year."

Chair:
"Is there a second?"

Any Member:
"Second."

Chair:
"It is moved and seconded that the department host an awards banquet at the end of the year."

"Is there any discussion?" (The chair should ask three times if needed)
(After discussion is finished)

Chair:
"Is there any further discussion?"

"Seeing none, we shall proceed to vote. All those in favor of the department hosting an awards banquet at the end of the year say aye. Those opposed say no."

"Motion passes. We shall host an awards banquet at the end of the year."

or

"Motion fails."

"Is there any further business?" or "What is the pleasure of the group."

Incidental Main Motions

A main motion that is incidental to or relates to the business of the chapter.

Adopt

Motion used to adopt (accept or agree to) a report or the recommendation of an officer or a committee which the group previously directed the officer or committee to prepare.

Member:

"I move to adopt the recommendation of the committee."

Ratify

Motion used to ratify (approve or confirm) an action already taken by officers, committees, or delegates in excess of their instructions — such as an emergency action taken by the officers.

Member:

"I move that the action taken by the officers dealing with the banquet ticket prices be ratified."

CHAPTER TWO
MOTIONS

Fill In The Blank Review

1. A _____ is a formal way of stating what you want to happen in a meeting.

2. Using correct motions will give you the ability to bring forth your _____ and opinions during meetings.

3. The _____ motion is used to bring business before the group.

4. A _____ motion is a type of motion that allows a group to deal directly with a main motion without voting on the main motion itself.

5. _____ motions do not relate to the pending question (motion).

6. Point of Order is an _____ motion.

7. An incidental motion relates to the _____ motion or other motions on the floor.

8. A main motion requires a _____ vote to pass.

9. To make a motion a member needs to rise and _____ the chairperson.

10. Before a members proposes a main motion he or she needs to be _____ by the chair.

11. After a main motion in made another member must _____ the motion before it can be discussed.

12. The _____ is the formal statement by the chairperson, of a proposed motion.

13. After a motion is stated to the group by the chairperson, the motion can be _____. (Note: some motions are not discussed)

14. A motion is voted on when there is no further _____.

15. A correct main motion example would be: "I move _____ the club hold a charity raffle in June."

16. A correct main motion example would be: "I move _____ send five members to the annual conference."

CHAPTER TW0
MOTIONS

Crossword Four
Clues on page 38

EclipseCrossword.com

CHAPTER TWO
MOTIONS

Crossword Four Clues

Across

4. Motion used to approve of an action already taken.

5. A formal way to state your idea in a meeting.

7. Number of motion groups.

8. Formal statement of a motion by the chairperson.

9. Can be discussed.

10. Motions that deal with matters of urgency.

Down

1. Type motion that allows the group to deal with a main motion before it is voted on.

2. Motion used to accept a report.

3. To bring your idea before the group use a _____ motion.

6. Type of motion that relates to the main motion.

CHAPTER TWO
MOTIONS

True/False Review Quiz Four

1. A motion is simply a formal way of saying what you want to happen in a meeting.

2. A main motion is a motion that brings business before the group.

3. Main motions can be made while other motions are pending.

4. "I motion that the club hold a charity raffle in June" is correct form for a main motion.

5. A subsidiary motion is a type of motion by which a group deals with other motions other than the main motion itself.

6. Refer to a Committee is a subsidiary motion.

7. Point of Order is a subsidiary motion.

8. A main motion cannot be amended.

9. Privileged motions relate to the pending question (motion).

10. Privileged motions are not debated (discussed).

11. A motion to adjourn is a privileged motion.

12. An incidental motion is a motion that relates to the main motion and other parliamentary motions.

13. A main motion is a motion that brings a question again before the assembly.

14. Reconsider is a motion that brings a question again before the assembly.

15. Motions that bring a question again before the assembly cannot be discussed or voted on.

CHAPTER THREE
Subsidiary Motions

A subsidiary motion is a type of motion by which a group deals directly with a main motion prior to, or instead of, voting on the main motion itself.

Postpone Indefinitely

This motion kills the main motion for the duration of the current meeting. It can be useful in getting rid of a bad main motion. It prevents any action from being taken on the main motion during the current meeting.

Details:

- **The maker of this motion must first be recognized by the chair.**
- **The motion is out of order when another person has the floor.**
- **Requires a second.**
- **Is debatable.**
- **Is not amendable.**
- **Majority vote.**
- **Can be reconsidered with an affirmative vote only. This means the motion to postpone indefinitely must have passed in order for it to be reconsidered.**

Member:

"I move that the motion to have an awards banquet be postponed indefinitely."

Any Member:

"Second."

Chair:

" It is moved and seconded that the motion to have an awards banquet be postponed indefinitely."

"Is there any discussion?"

After Discussion

Chair:

"All those in favor of the motion to postpone indefinitely, the motion to have an awards banquet, say aye. Those opposed say no."

Chair:

"Motion passes. The motion to have an awards banquet will be postponed indefinitely"

"Is there any further business?"

or

"What is the pleasure of the group.?"

or

"Motion fails. The motion to have an awards banquet will not be postponed indefinitely."

"Is there any further business?"

or

"What is the pleasure of the group?"

Amend

The motion to amend is used to modify or change a main motion. Usually it is used to add the details to a main motion such as time, location, etc. Amendments change the wording of a pending main motion before the pending motion itself is voted on. An amendment must also be germane - that is, it must be closely related to the main motion.

The first amendment to a main motion is called the primary amendment or the amendment to the first degree. An amendment to a primary amendment is called a secondary amendment or an amendment to the second degree. **Only one primary and one secondary amendment are allowed at one time.**

Each amendment is discussed and voted upon before the main motion is voted upon. If there are two amendments on the floor, one primary and one secondary, they are always discussed and voted on in the reverse order, i.e. amendment to the second degree, amendment to the first degree, main motion.

Details:
- **The maker of this motion must first be recognized by the chair.**
- **The motion is out of order when another person has the floor.**
- **Requires a second.**
- **Is debatable if the motion to be amended is debatable.**
- **Is amendable.**
- **Majority vote.**
- **Can be reconsidered.**

Methods of amending motions:

<u>Addition or Insertion</u>
Insert or add words, insert or add a paragraph

Striking Out
Strike out words, strike out a paragraph

Strike Our and Insert
Applies to words

Substitution
Strike out a paragraph and insert another

Examples:

Main Motion:

"I move that the department host an awards dinner at the end of the year."

Different Amendments that could be made by a member:

Example:

Member:
"I move to amend the main motion by <u>adding</u>, and the department managers will be in charge."

Chair:
"Is there a second?"

"It has been moved and seconded to amend the main motion by adding, and the department managers will be in charge."

"Is there any discussion?"

After discussion, the chair calls for a vote on the amendment. If the amendment passes, the main motion has been modified. If the amendment fails, the main motion stays as it was.

The chair asks for any further discussion on the main motion as modified or in its original form.

Example:

"The amendment passes. The main motion now reads that the department host an awards dinner at the end of the year and the department managers will be in charge."

"Is there any further discussion on the main motion?"

This process continues until the main motion is the way the members want it to be. Once there are no further amendments the chair calls for a final vote on the main motion.

More Example Amendments:

"I move to amend the main motion by <u>inserting</u> the word 'program' after awards."

"I move to amend the main motion by <u>striking out</u> the word 'awards' before banquet."

"I move to amend the main motion by <u>striking out</u> the word 'dinner' and <u>inserting</u> the word 'banquet'."

Refer to a Committee

This motion is used to send a pending motion to a small group or committee so that the motion can be carefully investigated and brought back at a later meeting to be considered by the members.

Details:
- **The maker of this motion must first be recognized by the chair.**
- **The motion is out of order when another person has the floor.**
- **Requires a second.**
- **Is debatable.**
- **Is amendable.**
- **Majority vote.**
- **Can be reconsidered if the assigned committee has not begun work on the matter.**

The necessary details of a motion to commit, which should be stated by the maker of the motion, are as follows:

Designate the committee chairperson or specify how to select one
State how to select the committee
State how many members will be on the committee
State when the committee will report back to the group
Assign the power to act *(Gives the committee the authority to do work on behalf of the organization)*

Example:
Member:
"I move to refer the motion to a committee of four, with Sue Jones as the chairperson, the members to be appointed by the chair, with the power to act, and to report back at the April meeting."

Chair:

"Is there a second?"

"Second."

"It has been properly moved and seconded to refer the motion to a committee of four, with Sue Jones as the chairperson, the members to be appointed by the chair, with the power to act, and to report back at the April meeting."

"Is there any discussion?"

(Discussion)

"All those in favor of the motion to refer please say aye. Those opposed say no."

"Motion passes or motion fails."

If the motion to refer to a committee passes, the committee would be set up as stated in the motion and the chairperson would ask if there was any further business to transact at the meeting. If the motion to refer were to fail, the chairperson would state that the motion has failed and go back to the main motion on the floor.

Postpone Definitely

This motion is used to postpone action on a pending motion to a definite day, time, meeting, or event in the future.

- **The maker of this motion must first be recognized by the chair.**
- **The motion is out of order when another person has the floor.**
- **Requires a second.**
- **Is debatable.**
- **Is amendable.**
- **Majority vote.**
- **Can be reconsidered.**

Member:

"I move to postpone the motion to have an awards banquet until the January department meeting."

Chair:

"Is there a second?"

"Second."

"It is moved and seconded to postpone the motion to have an awards banquet until the January department meeting."

"Is there any discussion?"

(Discussion)

"Seeing no further discussion we will proceed to vote."

"All those in favor please say aye."

"Those opposed say no."

"Motion passes. We will postpone the motion to have an awards banquet until the January department meeting."

or

"Motion fails. We will not postpone the motion."

Limit or Extend Limits of Debate

This motion is used to control debate on a pending motion.

Debate on a motion can be *limited* by:
Reducing the number of speeches.
Controlling the length of speeches.
Setting the specific time at which debate will be closed.

The motion can be used to *extend the limits* of debate by:
Allowing more speakers.
Allowing longer time for each speaker.

Details:

- **The maker of this motion must first be recognized by the chair.**

- **The motion is out of order when another person has the floor.**

- **Requires a second.**

- **Is not debatable.**

- **Is amendable.**

- **Two-thirds vote (rising vote required).**

- **Can be reconsidered.**

Depending on the desired outcome, there are several forms which you can use to make this motion . . .

To fix the hour for closing debate:
Member:

"I move that at 9:00 p.m. debate on the motion to . . . (state the pending motion) . . . be closed."

To limit the time spent in debate:

Member:

"I move that debate on the pending motion be limited to twenty minutes."

To limit the amount of time of debate for each speaker:

Member:

"I move to limit debate on the pending motion to five minutes per speaker."

To limit the number of speakers:

Member:

"I move to limit debate on the pending motion to three speakers."

To extend debate:

Member:

"I move that Miss Smith's time be extended 5 minutes."

Previous Question

The previous question is used to bring the assembly to an immediate vote on one or more pending motions. It immediately closes all debate and stops any further amendments.

In meetings, members will often call out, "Question!" This is not a correct motion and is simply an expression of opinion that a person is ready to vote.

Details:
- **The maker of this motion must first be recognized by the chair.**
- **The motion is out of order when another person has the floor.**
- **Requires a second.**
- **Is not debatable.**
- **Is not amendable.**
- **Two-thirds vote (rising vote required)**
- **Can be reconsidered.**

Member:
"I move the previous question."

"Second."

Chair:
"The previous question is moved on the motion to have an awards banquet."

"All those in favor of ordering the previous question, please rise."

"Be seated."

"Those opposed, please rise."   *"Be seated."*

If the motion on the previous question passes with a two-thirds vote, the chair immediately calls for a vote on the pending motion (awards banquet).

Chair:

"The motion for the previous question passes."

"All those in favor of the main motion to have an awards banquet say aye."

"Those opposed say no."

If the motion of the previous question fails, the chair announces the result and goes back to the pending main motion (awards banquet).

Chair:

"The motion on the previous question fails."

"Is there any further discussion on the main motion to have an awards banquet?"

Lay on the Table

This motion enables the assembly to lay a pending motion aside temporarily when something more urgent has arisen. There is no time set for taking the matter up again. Motions can be laid on the table up until the time the last vote is taken on a pending motion.

Details:

- **The maker of this motion must first be recognized by the chair.**
- **The motion is out of order when another person has the floor.**
- **Requires a second.**
- **Is not debatable.**
- **Is not amendable.**
- **Majority vote.**
- **Cannot be reconsidered.**

Member:
"I move to lay the motion on the table."

"Second."

Chair:
"It is moved and seconded to lay the motion to hold an awards banquet on the table."

"Those in favor say Aye."   *"Those opposed say No."*

"Motion passes. We will lay the motion to hold an awards banquet on the table." "What is the pleasure of the group."
    or
"Motion fails. We will not lay the motion to hold an awards banquet on the table." "Is there any more discussion on the main motion?"

CHAPTER THREE
SUBSIDIARY MOTIONS
Review Questions

1. Which motion kills the current main motion for the duration of the current meeting?

2. Can a motion to postpone indefinitely be amended?

3. Which motion can be used to change or modify another motion?

4. What does it mean to say that an amendment must be germane to the main motion?

5. Can an amendment be amended?

6. What is the first amendment to a main motion called?

7. How many amendments are allowed at one time?

8. What happens to a main motion if an amendment passes?

9. Which motion is used to send a pending motion to a small group or committee?

10. When can a motion to refer to a committee be reconsidered?

11. What does it mean to give a committee the power to act?

12. Which motion would you use if you wanted to postpone a motion until another day?

13. Which motion could you use if you wanted to control the amount of time each person can speak during a meeting?

14. What type of vote is needed for a motion to limit debate?

15. What motion can you use to bring the group (assembly) to a vote on a motion?

16. Why does a motion for the previous question require a rising vote?

17. When a motion is laid on the table is a time set to consider the motion again?

Crossword Five

Clues on page 56

CHAPTER THREE
SUBSIDIARY MOTIONS

Crossword Five Clues

Across

2. A motion for the previous _____ is used to bring the assembly to an immediate vote on a motion.

5. Type of vote required for the previous question.

8. Used to modify or change a main motion.

9. The first amendment.

12. Refer to a committee can be dealt with again.

14. A motion to postpone _____ can postpone a motion until a future day.

Down

1. To set a motion aside temporarily you can move to lay it on this.

3. Group of motions used to deal with a main motion.

4. An amendment of the second degree.

6. A motion to postpone _____ can get rid of a bad motion.

7. _____ debate is used to control debate on a motion.

10. Motion to send a pending motion to a committee.

11. A motion to limit debate cannot be _____.

13. Order that two amendments are voted on.

CHAPTER THREE
SUBSIDIARY MOTIONS

True/False Review Quiz Five

1. A subsidiary motion is a type of motion by which a group deals directly with a main motion prior to, or instead of, voting on the main motion itself.

2. Postpone indefinitely kills the main motion until the next motion is made.

3. Postpone indefinitely is in order when another person has the floor.

4. The motion to amend is used to modify or change a main motion.

5. A motion to amend must not be related to the main motion.

6. An amendment can be amended.

7. There can be up to three amendments on the floor.

8. Each amendment is discussed and voted upon after the main motion is voted upon.

9. Amendments are always discussed and voted on in the reverse order.

10. A motion to amend does not require a second.

11. A motion to refer to a committee is used to send a pending motion to a small group.

12. A motion to refer to a committee cannot be reconsidered.

13. Postpone definitely is used to postpone action on a pending motion to a definite day, time, meeting, or event in the future.

14. Postpone definitely requires a majority vote.

15. Limit debate is used to control debate on a pending motion.

16. Debate can be limited in a meeting, but debate cannot be extended.

17. A motion to limit debate requires a majority vote.

18. The previous question is used to bring the assembly to an immediate vote on one or more pending motions.

19. In a meeting a member can call out "question" when they wish to move the previous question.

20. With a motion to lay on the table there is a time and date set to take up the matter again.

CHAPTER FOUR
Privileged Motions

Privileged motions do not relate to the pending business, but they do relate to special matters of immediate importance.

Call for the Orders of the Day

Motion by which a member can require the assembly to conform to its agenda, program, or order of business.

Details:
- **The maker of this motion does not need to be recognized by the chair.**
- **The motion is in order when another person has the floor.**
- **Does not require a second.**
- **Is not debatable.**
- **Is not amendable.**
- **Requires a two-thirds negative vote not to follow the orders of the day.**
- **Cannot be reconsidered.**

When the orders of the day are called for the chair should immediately announce the business or subject that is in order from the agenda.

A vote should then be taken by the chair. It requires a two-thirds negative rising vote not to follow the orders of the day. In other words, if two-thirds of the members vote against a call for the orders of the day, then the order of business does not have to be followed.

Member:
"Mr. President, I call for the orders of the day."

Chair:

"The orders of the day are called for."

"The orders of the day are to . . ." *(read item from the agenda)*

"All those in favor of conforming to the orders of the day please rise."

"Those opposed, please rise."

"Motion passes. We shall conform to the orders of the day."

Motion fails. We shall not conform to the orders of the day."

If the motion for the orders of the day passes

Chair:

"What is the pleasure of the group pertaining to the orders of the day?"

Question of Privilege

This motion permits a member to make a special request at a meeting. There are two kinds of questions of privilege: (1) those relating to the whole assembly; and (2) those relating to questions of personal privilege. The question of privilege is dealt with immediately by the chairperson.

Details:

- **The maker of this motion does not need to be recognized by the chair.**
- **The motion is in order when another member has the floor if the situation being addressed by the question of privilege is urgent. If the item is not urgent, a motion for a question of privilege should not be made while another member is speaking.**
- **The motion is in order when another person has the floor, but should not interrupt a speaker.**
- **Does not require a second.**
- **Is not debatable.**
- **Is not amendable.**
- **No vote. The question of privilege is ruled upon by the chair.**
- **Cannot be reconsidered.**

Question of Personal Privilege

Member:
"Madam President, I rise to a question of personal privilege."

Chair:
"Please state your question."

Member:
"Can we please open the window? I am feeling too hot."

Chair:

"Yes, please feel free to open the window."

Question of Privilege Relating to the Assembly

Member:

"Madam President, I rise to a question of privilege affecting the assembly."

Chair:

"Please state your question."

Member:

"Madam President, I think people are having trouble hearing. Can we turn up the volume on the PA system?"

Chair:

"Yes. Mr. Clark, will you please turn up the volume on the PA system."

Recess

This motion may be used by any member to bring about a short intermission in the meeting.

Details:

- **The maker of this motion must first be recognized by the chair.**
- **The motion is not in order when another person has the floor.**
- **Requires a second.**
- **Is not debatable.**
- **Is amendable.**
- **Majority vote.**
- **Cannot be reconsidered.**

Member:

"Mr. Chairman, I move to take a five minute recess."

Chair:

"Is there a second?"

"Second."

"It has been moved and seconded to take a five minute recess."

"Are there any amendments to this motion?"

If there are amendments made the chair must deal with these. After the amendments are disposed of, or if there are no amendments, the chair calls for a vote.

"All those if favor of the motion to take a five minute recess, please say aye."

"Those opposed say no."

"The ayes have it and the meeting stands recessed for five minutes."

What to do at the end of the Recess

After the recess time has expired the chair must regain control of the meeting and resume where the assembly left off.

Chair:
Two taps of the gavel.
"The meeting will come to order."
"The time of recess has expired. We were discussing the motion to ..."
"What is the pleasure of the group?"

Adjourn

Motion used to close the meeting -- may be used by any member.

Details:
- **The maker of this motion must first be recognized by the chair.**
- **The motion is not in order when another person has the floor.**
- **Requires a second.**
- **Is not debatable.**
- **Is not amendable.**
- **Majority vote.**
- **Cannot be reconsidered.**

Member:
"Madam president, I move to adjourn the meeting."

"Second."

Chair:
"It has been moved and seconded to adjourn the meeting."

"All those in favor of adjourning the meeting say aye."

"Those opposed say no."

"Motion passes, the meeting is adjourned."

or

Chair:
"It has been moved and seconded to adjourn the meeting. If there is no objection, the meeting will now adjourn. (Pause) Since there is no objection, the meeting is adjourned." Close the meeting with one tap of the gavel.

Fix the Time to Which to Adjourn

The purpose of this motion is to set the time, and sometimes the place, for another meeting to continue the business of the current session. This motion has no effect on when the present meeting will adjourn.

Details:

- **The maker of this motion must first be recognized by the chair.**
- **The motion is not in order when another person has the floor.**
- **Requires a second.**
- **Is not debatable.**
- **Is amendable.**
- **Majority vote.**
- **Can be reconsidered.**

Member:
"Mr. Chairman, I move that when this meeting adjourns, it stand adjourned to meet Tuesday, March 12, at 7:00 p.m. at the department meeting room."

"Second."

Chair:
"It is moved and seconded to fix the time to which to adjourn so that when we adjourn, we stand adjourned until 7:00 p.m. on Tuesday, March 12, at the department meeting room."

"Are there any amendments to this motion?"
(The chair must deal with any amendments)

"All those in favor of the motion to fix the time to which to adjourn so that when we adjourn, we stand adjourned until 7:00 p.m. on Tuesday, March 12, at the department meeting room, say aye."

"Those opposed say no."

"The ayes have it. When we adjourn, we will stand adjourned until 7:00 p.m. on Tuesday, March 12, at the department meeting room."

CHAPTER FOUR
PRIVILEGED MOTIONS

Review Questions

1. Do privileged motions relate to the pending business?

2. Which motion can a member use to require the assembly to conform to its agenda, program, or order of business.

3. What type of vote does a call for the orders of the day require?

4. Which motion permits a member to make a special request at a meeting.

5. When is a question of privilege in order when another person has the floor?

6. Which motion would you use to request a short intermission during a meeting?

7. Which motion would you use if you want to close a meeting?

8. What is the purpose of the motion to fix the time to which to adjourn?

9. Does a motion to fix the time to which to adjourn effect the adjournment of the current meeting?

10. Can a motion to fix the time to which to adjourn be reconsidered?

CHAPTER FOUR
PRIVILEGED MOTIONS

Crossword Six
Clues on page 70

CHAPTER FOUR
PRIVILEGED MOTIONS

Crossword Six Clues

Across

4. Motion to close a meeting.

5. Call for the orders of the day is not.

6. Call for intermission.

7. Fix the _____ to which to adjourn.

9. Use a question of _____ to make a special request during a meeting.

11. Call for the orders of the day does not require this.

12. Call for the orders of the day requires a two-thirds _____ vote not to follow the orders of the day.

Down

1. Cannot do this with a call for the orders of the day.

2. A question of privilege for a personal matter should be this.

3. Call for the orders of the day is in _____ when another person has the floor.

4. Call for the orders of the day is not _____.

8. A motion to call for the orders of the day requires the group to conform to this.

9. These motions do not relate to the pending business.

10. You don't need to do this with a question of privilege.

CHAPTER FOUR
PRIVILEGED MOTIONS

True/False Review Quiz Six

1. Privileged motions relate to the pending business.

2. A motion to call for the orders of the day is amendable.

3. The purpose of a motion to call for the orders of the day is to require the group top follow its agenda.

4. A motion to call for the orders of the day requires a majority vote.

5. A question of privilege does not require a vote.

6. A question of privilege can be debated.

7. A motion for recess is in order when another person has the floor.

8. A motion to adjourn can only be used by special members.

9. Fix the time to which to adjourn is a motion used to adjourn the current meeting.

10. A motion to fix the time to which to adjourn requires a two-thirds vote.

CHAPTER FIVE
Incidental Motions

Incidental motions relate to the pending business. As a class, incidental motions deal with questions of procedure. An incidental motion is said to be *incidental* to the motion or matter out of which it arises. In other words, an incidental motion could accompany another motion, but not be a part of it. Incidental motions usually relate to the main motion in such a way that they must be decided immediately before business can proceed.

Point of Order

This motion can be used when a member thinks the rules of the assembly have been violated.

Details:
- **The maker of this motion does not need to be recognized by the chair.**
- **The motion is in order when another person has the floor.**
- **Does not require a second.**
- **Is not debatable.**
- **Is not amendable.**
- **No vote. Is responded to by the chair.**
- **Cannot be reconsidered.**

Member:
"I rise to a point of order." or "Point of order."

Chair: *"State your point."*

Member:

"The motion on the floor did not receive a second."

Chair:

"Point well taken. Is there a second on the motion to hold an awards banquet?"

After the member states his or her point, the chair rules on whether the point of order is well taken or is not well taken, and briefly explains the reasoning for the conclusion.

Appeal

This motion gives a member a device to use when disagreeing with a ruling by the chair.

Details:

- **The maker of this motion does not need to be recognized by the chair.**

- **The motion is in order when another person has the floor.**
- **Requires a second.**
- **Is debatable.**
- **Is not amendable.**
- **Majority in negative required to reverse the chair's decision. In other words, a majority of the members must vote against the chair's decision in order to reverse it.**
- **Can be reconsidered.**

The appeal must be made at the time a ruling is made by the chair. If any business or debate has occurred after the ruling by the chair, it is too late to appeal.

Member:
"I appeal from the decision of the chair."

"Second."

Chair:
"The chair's decision regarding the time of the next meeting has been appealed. The question is, shall the decision of the chair be sustained? All those in favor of sustaining the chair's decision say aye, those opposed say no."

"The ayes have it, the chair's decision is sustained."

or

"The noes have it, the chair's decision is not sustained."

Suspend the Rules

This motion is used when the assembly wishes to do something that violates one or more of its regular rules.

Details:
- **The maker of this motion must first be recognized by the chair.**
- **The motion is out of order when another person has the floor.**
- **Requires a second.**
- **Is not debatable.**
- **Is not amendable.**
- **Two-thirds vote.**
- **Cannot be reconsidered.**

Member:
"I move to suspend the standing rule requiring managers to wear ties at meetings."

"Second."

Chair:
"All those in favor of suspending the standing rule requiring managers to wear ties at meeting please rise."

"Those opposed please rise."

"The motion passes. We will suspend the standing rule requiring managers to wear ties to meetings."

or

"The motion fails. We will not suspend the standing rule requiring managers to wear ties to meetings."

Objection to the Consideration of a Question

This motion is used to enable the assembly to avoid a particular main motion. The objection must be made before there has been any debate on the main motion.

Details:

- **The maker of this motion does not need to be recognized by the chair.**
- **The motion is in order when another person has the floor.**
- **Must be moved before debate has begun on the pending motion.**
- **Does not require a second.**
- **Is not debatable.**
- **Is not amendable.**
- **Two-thirds vote against consideration of the pending motion sustains the objection.**

A two-thirds vote against consideration of a main motion is required to sustain the objection. If an objection to the consideration of a question (motion) is sustained, the main motion is dismissed for the duration of the meeting.

Member:
"I object to the consideration of the question."

Chair:
"The consideration of the question is objected to. Shall the question be considered? Those in favor of considering the main motion to have an awards banquet please rise. Those opposed, please rise."

"The affirmative has it, the objection is not sustained. We shall consider the main motion to have an awards banquet."

or

"The negative has it, the objection is sustained. The main motion to have an awards banquet is dismissed."

If two-thirds vote no, then the objection is sustained and the main motion is dismissed. If less than two-thirds are opposed then the objection is not sustained and the main motion will be brought before the assembly.

Division of a Question

When a motion relating to a single subject contains several parts, the parts can be separated to be discussed and voted on as distinct motions. The motion for division of a question can be applied to a main motion or an amendment. It cannot be made to a main motion when an amendment is pending. The motion to divide can be made anytime during the consideration of a motion.

Details:
- **The maker of this motion must first be recognized by the chair.**
- **The motion is out of order when another person has the floor.**
- **Requires a second.**
- **Is not debatable.**
- **Is amendable.**
- **Majority vote.**
- **Cannot be reconsidered.**

Example main motion on the floor:
To hold an awards banquet and finance the cost with a fundraiser.

Member:
"I move to divide the question (or motion) such that the awards banquet and fundraiser are considered separately."

Chair:
"Is there a second?"

"Second."

"All those in favor of dividing the question such that the awards banquet and the fundraiser be considered separately say aye."

"Those opposed say no."

"The ayes have it, we will divide the question."

Each part is then discussed and voted on separately.

Chair:
"Is their any discussion on the first motion stating that we have an awards banquet?"

or

"The noes have it, we will not divide the question."

"Is there any further discussion on the main motion that states we have an awards banquet and finance the cost with a fundraiser?"

Division of the Assembly (House)

If a member believes that a voice or hand vote was not accurate a division of the house motion may be called for. This motion requires the chair to call for a rising vote (members stand). A rising vote is not counted unless the chair believes it is necessary or if a member demands it by making a motion to count the vote. A motion demanding a count must receive a second and a majority vote. Example: *"I move that the vote be counted."*

Details:
- **The maker of this motion does not need to be recognized by the chair.**
- **The motion is in order when another person has the floor.**
- **Does not require a second.**
- **Is not debatable.**
- **Is not amendable.**
- **The demand of a single member requires the chair to call for a rising vote.**
- **Cannot be reconsidered.**

A member may simply call out:

"Division of the house!"   or   *"Division!"*

Chair:

"A division is called for."

"All those in favor of the motion to have an awards banquet please rise."

(Count the affirmative vote and report to the secretary)

"Those opposed please stand."
(Count the negative vote and report to the secretary)

The chair should report the final vote count to the assembly and the result of the rising vote.

Example:

"Ten in favor and five against. The affirmative has it. We shall hold an awards banquet."

Parliamentary Inquiry

A parliamentary inquiry is a question directed to the presiding officer to obtain information on a matter of parliamentary law pertaining to the business at hand.

Details:
- **The maker of this motion does not need to be recognized by the chair.**
- **The motion is in order when another person has the floor.**
- **Does not require a second.**
- **Is not debatable.**
- **Is not amendable.**
- **No vote. Is responded to by the chair.**
- **Cannot be reconsidered.**

Member:
"Madam President, I rise to a parliamentary inquiry."

Chair:
"The member will state his or her inquiry." or "State your inquiry."

Member:
"Does a motion to suspend the rules require a two-thirds majority vote?"

The chair answers the question or refers it to the Parliamentarian.

Point of Information

This is a request directed to the chair for information relevant to the business at hand, but not related to parliamentary procedure. Use a *parliamentary inquiry* for questions about proper procedure during a meeting.

Details:
- **The maker of this motion does not need to be recognized by the chair.**
- **The motion is in order when another person has the floor and if it requires immediate attention.**
- **Does not require a second.**
- **Is not debatable.**
- **Is not amendable.**
- **No vote. Is responded to by the chair.**
- **Cannot be reconsidered.**

Member:
"Mr. Chairman, I rise to a point of information."

Chair:
"The member will state her point."

Member:
"Will the conference hall be big enough for the awards banquet?"

After the member states her point, the chair provides the requested information.

If a member is requesting information from a member who is speaking, the inquirer can use the following form:

Member:
"Madam President, will the member yield for a question?"

Withdraw or Modify a Motion

Before a motion has been stated by the chair

Before a motion has been stated by the chair, it is the property of the person who made it. The maker of a motion can withdraw it or modify it without the consent of anyone. Another member may also ask if the maker of the motion is willing to withdraw a motion or accept modification to it.

Details:
- **A member does not need to be recognized by the chair to withdraw or modify a motion before it has been stated to the assembly by the chair.**
- **The motion is in order when another person has the floor.**
- **Does not require a second.**
- **Is not debatable.**
- **Is not amendable.**
- **No vote required.**
- **Cannot be reconsidered.**

Member:
Main Motion: *"I move that we hold an awards banquet and have the department managers be in charge."*

To Withdraw A Motion

Member: *"Mr. President, I withdraw the motion".*

Chair: *"The motion has been withdrawn."*

To Modify a Motion

Member:
"Mr. President, I wish to modify the motion by striking out 'and the department managers be in charge'."

Chair:
"The motion now reads that we hold an awards banquet."

After a motion has been stated by the chair

After a motion has been stated by the chair it belongs to the assembly. The maker of the motion must *request permission* to withdraw or modify the motion. A request for permission to withdraw a motion can be made at any time before voting on the question has begun. If a motion is withdrawn, all other motions and amendments adhering to the motion are dropped. A withdrawn motion is not recorded in the minutes by the secretary.

Details:
- **Is in order when another person has the floor.**
- **Requires a second if the motion to withdraw or modify was made by the mover of the original motion.**
- **Does not require a second if the motion to withdraw or modify is made by another person.**
- **Is not debatable.**
- **Is not amendable.**
- **Majority vote.**
- **A motion to withdraw can be reconsidered only when there was a negative vote.**
- **A motion to modify can be reconsidered.**

Member:

"Madam President, I ask permission to withdraw the motion."

The chair can handle this motion by unanimous consent. If no one objects, the motion is withdrawn or modified.

Chair:

"Unless there is objection, (pause) the motion is withdrawn."

If there is objection, the motion to withdraw or modify must be voted on. It requires a majority vote.

Chair:

"All those in favor of allowing the motion to be withdrawn say 'aye', those opposed say 'no'."

"The ayes have it. The motion is withdrawn."

CHAPTER FIVE
INCIDENTAL MOTIONS

Review Questions

1. What kind of business do incidental motions relate to?

2. Can incidental motions be part of another motion?

3. What does it mean to say that incidental motions take precedence over other pending motions?

4. Which motion can you use if you think the rules of the assembly (group) have been violated?

5. Does a point of order require a vote?

6. What type of vote is required to reverse the chair's decision?

7. When is it too late to appeal the chair's decision?

8. What is the purpose of a motion to suspend the rules?

9. What is the purpose of an objection to the consideration of a question?

10. What happens if an objection to the consideration of a question is sustained?

11. When a motion contains several parts can they be separated and considered separately?

12. What motion is used to separate the parts of a question?

13. What can you do if you believe the results of a voice vote were not accurate?

14. What should you do if you have a question about parliamentary procedure during a meeting?

15. Who answers questions about parliamentary procedure during a meeting?

17. Which motion can you use to ask a question during a meeting?

18. If you have made a motion when can you withdraw it?

Crossword Seven

Clues on page 91

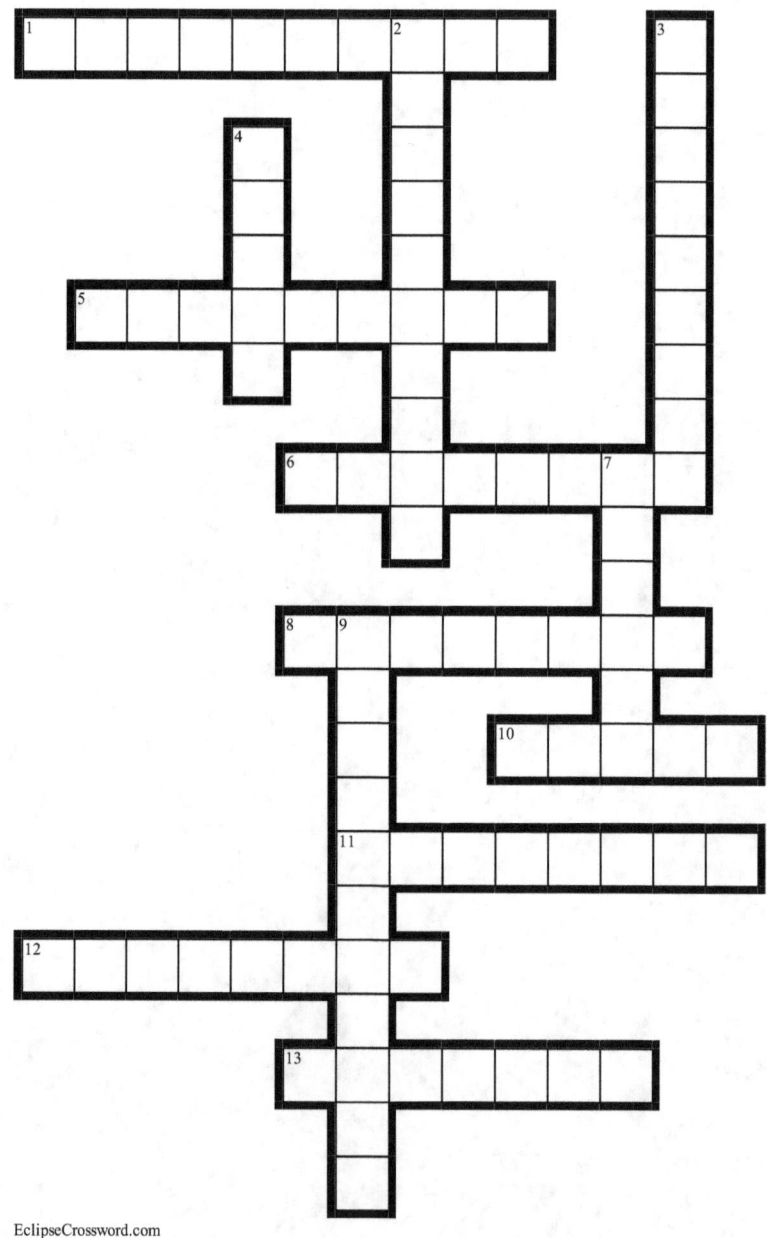

CHAPTER FIVE
INCIDENTAL MOTIONS

Crossword Seven Clues

Across

1. You must get this to withdraw your motion if it has already be stated by the chair.

5. Division of a question can be used to divide the parts of a main motion and an _____.

6. This person responds to a parliamentary inquiry.

8. A motion to suspend the rules is used when the assembly wishes to do something that _____ the regular rules.

10. Use a point of order when you think these have been violated.

11. Motion you can use if you believe a voice vote was not accurate.

12. Before your motion is stated by the chair you can do this.

13. A majority vote in the negative is required to do this to a chairperson's decision.

Down

2. Motions that deal with questions of procedure.

3. Motion used to enable the assembly to avoid a particular main motion.

4. Use a _____ of information to request information relevant to the current business.

7. Use this motion when you disagree with a ruling by the chair.

9. When incidental motions should be decided.

CHAPTER FIVE
INCIDENTAL MOTIONS

True/False Review Quiz Seven

1. Incidental motions do not relate to the pending business.

2. An incidental motion could accompany another motion.

3. Incidental motions do not relate to the main motion.

4. A parliamentary inquiry is used when a member thinks the rules of the assembly have been violated.

5. A member who rises to a point of order does not need to be recognized by the chair.

6. A point of order is in order when another person has the floor.

7. Use an appeal if you disagree with a ruling by the chair.

8. An appeal can be amended.

9. An appeal is debatable.

10. A motion to suspend the rules is used when the assembly wishes to do something that violates one or more of its regular rules.

11. A motion to suspend the rules requires a majority vote.

12. An objection to the consideration of a question cannot be used to avoid a main motion.

13. The maker of an objection to the consideration of a question must be recognized by the chair.

14. A two-thirds vote against consideration of a main motion is required to sustain an objection to the consideration of a question.

15. When a motion relating to a single subject contains several parts, the parts can be separated to be discussed and voted on as distinct motions.

16. The motion used to divide a main motion (question) is called division of a question.

17. Division of the house (assembly) requires the chair to call for a voice vote.

18. A member may move to have a rising vote counted.

19. A parliamentary inquiry is a question directed to the presiding officer dealing with a personal matter of a member.

20. A parliamentary inquiry requires a majority vote.

21. A point of information is a request directed to the chair for information relevant to the business at hand, but not related to parliamentary procedure.

22. Before a motion has been stated by the chair it can be withdrawn by the maker of the motion.

23. The maker of a motion must be recognized by the chair in order to withdraw or modify a motion before it has been stated to the assembly by the chair.

CHAPTER SIX
Motions that Bring a Question Again Before the Assembly

Take From the Table

This motion is used to bring a previously tabled motion back for consideration by the assembly.

Details:
- **The maker of this motion must first be recognized by the chair.**
- **The motion is out of order when another person has the floor.**
- **Requires a second.**
- **Not debatable.**
- **Not amendable.**
- **Majority Vote.**
- **Cannot be reconsidered.**

Member:
"I move to take from the table the motion to have a fund raiser which was tabled at our last meeting."

Chair: *"Is there a second?"*

"Second."

"It has been properly moved a seconded to take from the table the motion to have a fund raiser which was tabled at our last meeting."

Chair:

"All those in favor of taking from the table, the motion to have a fund raiser which was tabled at our last meeting, say aye."

"Those opposed say no."

"The ayes have it. We will take from the table the motion to have a fund raiser which was tabled at our last meeting. Is there any discussion on this motion?"

or

"The motion fails. We will not take this motion from the table."

"Is there any further business?"

Rescind

The motion to rescind is used to strike out an entire main motion, resolution, rule, by-law, section, or paragraph, which was adopted at a previous meeting.

Details:

- **The maker of this motion must first be recognized by the chair.**
- **The motion is out of order when another person has the floor.**
- **Requires a second.**
- **Is debatable.**
- **Is amendable.**
- **Majority vote when notice of intent to make the motion is given at the previous meeting.**

or

- **Majority of the <u>entire</u> membership without previous notice.**

or

- **Two-thirds vote without previous notice.**
- **Can be reconsidered only when a negative vote occurred.**

Previous Notice - An announcement that the motion will be introduced must be made at the preceding meeting or must be included in the call for the meeting at which the motion will be brought up.

Member:
"I move to rescind the previously adopted main motion concerning the landscaping of the office grounds."

Chair:
"Is there a second?"

"Second."

"It has been properly moved and seconded to rescind the previously adopted main motion concerning the landscaping of the office grounds."

"Is there any discussion on this motion?"

(Discussion)

"All those in favor of the motion to rescind, please say aye."

"Those opposed please say no."

"The motion passes. The motion to landscape the office grounds is rescinded."

or

"The motion fails. We will not rescind the motion to landscape the office grounds."

Reconsider

A call for a motion to reconsider allows a motion which has already been voted on to be brought back for further consideration. This motion may only be made by a member who voted on the prevailing side. In other words, the member calling for the motion must have voted in favor of the original motion if it passed, or against it if the original motion failed.

Details:

- **The maker of this motion must first be recognized by the chair and must have voted on the prevailing side of the motion in question.**

- **The motion is out of order when another person has the floor.**
- **Requires a second.**
- **Debatable - if the motion proposed to be reconsidered is debatable.**
- **Not amendable.**
- **Majority vote.**
- **Cannot be reconsidered.**

Member:
"I move to reconsider the motion to hold our annual awards banquet in May voted on at the March meeting. I voted for (or against) this motion." (Must have been on the prevailing , winning, side.)

Chair:
"Is there a second."   Second."

"It has been moved and seconded to reconsider the motion to hold our annual awards banquet in May which was voted on at our March meeting."

"Is there any discussion?"   (The chair would ask for debate only if the motion to be reconsidered is debatable).

"All those in favor please say aye."

"Those opposed say no."

"Motion passes. We will reconsider the motion to hold our annual awards banquet in May."

"Is there any discussion on this motion?"

or

"The motion to reconsider fails. We will not reconsider this motion."

Motions that are Not Debatable
but can be Amended

There are four motions which cannot be debated or discussed, but they can be amended.

The four motions are:

Limit debate
Recess
Fix the time to which to adjourn
Division of a question

The chairperson should ask for amendments when any of these four motions are made in a meeting. The chairperson does not ask for discussion.

Example:

Member:
"I move to take a ten minute recess."

"Second."

Chair:
"It is moved and seconded to take a ten-minute recess. Are there any amendments to this motion?"

If there are no amendments, the chair calls for a vote on the motion. If amendments are made by the members, the chair must deal with these first.

CHAPTER SIX
MOTIONS THAT BRING A QUESTION AGAIN BEFORE THE ASSEMBLY

Review Questions

1. What are the three motions that bring a question again before the assembly?

2. Which motion does a motion to take from the table bring back for discussion?

3. Which motion would you use to strike out a motion which was adopted at a previous meeting?

4. What does "Previous Notice" mean?

5. What type of vote is required for a motion to rescind when previous notice is given?

6. What type of vote is required for a motion to rescind when previous notice is not given?

7. When can a motion to rescind be reconsidered?

8. Which motion allows a motion which has already been voted on to be brought back for further consideration.

9. Which members at a meeting can make a motion to reconsider?

10. What condition has to exist for a motion to reconsider to be debated?

CHAPTER SIX
MOTIONS THAT BRING A QUESTION
AGAIN BEFORE THE ASSEMBLY

True/False Review Quiz Eight

1. Take from the table is a motion used to bring a postponed motion back for further discussion.

2. Take from the table can be reconsidered.

3. A motion to rescind cannot strike out an entire main motion.

4. Previous notice refers to the minutes of a previous meeting.

5. A motion to rescind allows a majority vote as long as previous notice was given.

6. A motion to rescind can be reconsidered only when a negative vote occurred.

7. A call for a motion to reconsider allows a motion which has already been voted on to be brought back for further consideration.

8. A motion to reconsider can be made by any member at a meeting.

9. A member calling for the motion to reconsider must have voted in favor of the original motion if it passed, or against it if the original motion failed.

10. A motion to reconsider can be reconsidered.

CHAPTER SEVEN
Discussion Techniques

Discussion and debate on a motion is a very important step in the process of conducting business. It is extremely important to be able to present your ideas and opinions to the group in a clear and concise manner. Once a motion is on the floor individuals will have the opportunity to present their arguments on either side of the motion. Having the ability to persuade the group one way or the other will determine if a motion passes or fails. The following examples are provided in order to give the reader some phrases that may be useful during a business meeting.

"Members, I would encourage you to rescind this motion for two very good reasons."
"Number one..."
"Number two..."
"For these reasons I urge you to rescind this motion."

"Fellow members, there are three main reasons why I proposed this amendment to our main motion."
"First of all ..."
"Second of all..."
"And the third reason I proposed this amendment is that ..."
"For these reasons I hope that you will all vote yes for this amendment."
"I feel that this is a very strong amendment."
"I hope that you will vote in favor of this amendment."
or
"I hope that you will vote against this amendment."

"Fellow members I am very frustrated with the views of the previous speaker..."

"Therefore, I hope that you will all vote with me and vote no on this motion."

"I proposed this motion to refer because..."

"I totally disagree with the views of the previous speaker."

"I am very much in favor of this motion because..."

"I agree with the views of the previous speaker because..."

"For these reasons I hope that you will adopt this motion."

CHAPTER EIGHT
Nominating and Electing Officers

Nominations

Nominations are simply the process of selecting individuals to run for officer, board member, or committee member positions in an organization. Nominations can be made by the following methods:

- **Nominations from the floor or open nominations.**

- **Nominations by the chair.**

- **Nominations by a nominating committee.**

- **Nominations by ballot.**

- **Nominations by mail.**

- **Nominations by petition.**

Nominations from the Floor/Open Nominations

With open nominations the chair calls for nominations at the time designated by the organization. This is the most common method of nominating people in most organizations.

Rules for open nominations:
- ✓ A member does not need to be recognized by the chair to make a nomination.
- ✓ The member should rise when making the nomination.

✓ Does not require a second, however, another member may second a nomination to indicate their approval of the individual being nominated.
✓ No one can nominate more than one person for an office until all members wishing to make a nomination have had a chance to do so.
✓ The same person can be nominated for more than one office.
✓ If present, the person nominated can select which office they want to accept.
✓ If absent, the members can vote for which office the person will receive.

How to open nominations from the floor:

Chair:
"Nominations are now open for the office of President."

Member:
"Mr. Chairman, I nominate Susan."

Chair:
"Susan is nominated. Are there any further nominations for the office of President?"

Nominations by the Chair

The chair does not normally make nominations for officer positions. The chair can make nominations for committee membership and similar positions within the organization.

Nominations by Committee

A nominating committee is selected in advance to develop a list of nominations for officer, board member, or committee members that will be elected at a future meeting.

Rules for nominating committees:

- ✓ The committee should be elected by the membership or appointed by the executive board (officers).
- ✓ The committee can nominate one or more than one candidate for each office.
- ✓ Members of the committee can become nominees themselves.
- ✓ The committee should contact each person they decide to nominate in advance of the actual officer election day.

Report of nominations by the nominating committee:
The membership of an organization can be informed of the nominations prior to the election meeting by means of email, text message, mail, phone calls, etc. The nominating committee can report its list of nominees at a regular meeting. The nominating committee chairperson rises and presents the report as follows:

Nominating Committee Chairperson:
"Mr. President, the Nominating Committee submits the following nominations: For President, Ms. Jones; for Vice President, Mr. Smith; etc.

The nominating committee is automatically discharged when its nomination report is presented to the members at a meeting. If a nominee drops out, the committee will be considered still active in order to find a replacement nominee.

After the nominating committee has presented its report, the chair should call for further nominations from the floor.

Nominations by Ballot

A nominating ballot is given to each member. Each member votes for those individuals they wish to nominate for each particular office or position. Each member receiving a vote is nominated. A member who uses a ballot to nominate individuals does not have the right to make any nominations from the floor.

Nominations by Mail

This method can be useful when the members of an organization are wide spread and will not be together in time for nominations to take place. A ballot is usually mailed to the members with instructions for completing and returning it to the secretary.

Elections

The election voting process can be accomplished by any means that is accepted by the members of the organization. The most widely used method for elections in organized groups, boards, or clubs, is the ballot election process.

Ballot Elections

With a ballot election each voting member receives a piece of paper indicating the nominees for each office or position to be filled. Individuals, tellers, should be identified in advance to distribute, collect, and count the ballots. To maintain secrecy each ballot should be folded in a manner explained before the election process begins. After all ballots have been collected, the polls can be closed by a motion by a member and a two-thirds vote or they can be closed by the chair.

See the sample ballot on the next page.

Officer Election Ballot

Write the number corresponding to each office by the person's name who you feel should be elected to that office. Vote for only one person for each office or your ballot will be rejected.

President 6, Vice President 5, Secretary 4, Treasurer 3

Nominees:

Sue Jones   _____
Tim Black   _____
Larry Clark   _____
Jerry Smith   _____
Julie White   _____
Kathy Brown   _____
Bobby Woods   _____
Rick Blaire   _____
Joanna Barnes   _____

After collecting all of the ballots, add of the points for each candidate. The candidate with the most points would be president and so on.

CHAPTER NINE
Bylaws

Bylaws

The bylaws of an organization are the rules that govern the functions of the organization. In most organizations today, the constitution and by-laws are combined in one single document and referred to as the by-laws. The bylaws should provide a clear description of the objective of the organization, and the rights and duties of its members.

Content of the Bylaws

The bylaws should contain articles or sections that describe the name, object, members, officers, and the necessary details of how the organization will function.

The following bylaws and articles are a good example to follow when writing the bylaws for an organization.

STANDARD FORM FOR KEY CLUB BYLAWS

ARTICLE I: Name

Section 1. The name of this organization shall be the Key Club of

_____.

ARTICLE II: Organization

Section 1. Its form of organization, its ideals, and its purpose shall be similar to those of the Kiwanis Club of

_____.

(Kiwanis Club Sponsor)

Section 2. It shall be sponsored by, but not a part of, Kiwanis club of

_____. The Kiwanis Club assumes all chartering costs.

ARTICLE III: Objects and Activities

Section 1. The objects of the Key Club shall be:

· To develop initiative and leadership.
· To provide experience in living and working together.
· To serve the school and community.
· To cooperate with the school principal.
· To prepare for useful citizenship.

To accept and promote the following ideals:
To give primacy to the human and spiritual, rather than to the material values of life. To encourage the daily living of the Golden Rule in all human relationships.
To promote the adoption and application of higher standards in scholarship, sportsmanship, and social contacts.
To develop, by precept and example, a more intelligent, aggressive, and serviceable citizenship.
To provide a practical means to form enduring friendships, to render unselfish service, and to build better communities.

To cooperate in creating and maintaining that sound public opinion and high idealism which make possible the in- crease of righteousness, justice, patriotism, and good will.

Section 2. The activities of the Key Club shall be in accord with its Objects. They should include those suggested by Key Club International, plus such additional activities as might be adopted by the Key Club and approved by the school principal.

ARTICLE IV: Motto

Section 1. The motto of the Key Club shall be "Caring-Our Way of Life."

ARTICLE V: Membership

Section 1. Membership shall be limited to the high school students as apportioned from the senior, junior, sophomore, and freshmen classes by the Board of Directors, who possess the qualifications prescribed by Article 6, Section 1 of the Constitution of Key Club International.

ARTICLE VI: Officers

Section 1. Officers shall be president, vice-president, secretary, treasurer, editor, and webmaster or technology associated position and one director from each class. They shall serve for one (1) year or until their successors are elected and qualify.

Section 2. Each officer shall be a member in good standing. No other restrictions or limitations shall be placed on these officers.

Section 3. There shall be a Board of Directors, composed of the above officers and one director to be elected from each class.

Section 4. The duties of the officers shall be such as are usually performed by similar office holders, and as outlined by the Key Club International document "Duties of Club Officers."

Section 5. The Board of Directors shall approve the budget, approve all bills, take counsel with committees, discipline members, review and report to Kiwanis the performance of the club officers, and perform such other duties as shall be referred to it by the club, in compliance with these Bylaws and the requirements of Key Club International.

Section 6. All action by the club and the Board of Directors shall be subject to the approval of the principal and the sponsoring Kiwanis club. The Board of Directors shall meet at least once monthly at a time and place selected by the Board.

Section 7. Any general member may recommend the removal of a club officer to the Board of Directors. The Board of Directors shall hold a meeting at which the officer in question shall be heard. If approved, the recommendation shall be presented to the club and voted on by 2/3 vote of the quorum. In the event any officer should be re-moved from office, the officer shall be notified in writing by the secretary.

Section 8. The Faculty and Kiwanis Advisors shall serve as ex-officio members of the club Board of Directors, retaining all rights of that membership without the right to vote.

ARTICLE VII: Election of Officers

Section 1. Election of new officers (president, vice-president, secretary, treasurer, and editor) should be held at a meeting in February and they should take office in May.

Section 2. Election of directors (one from each class) shall be held at the first meeting following the opening of school in the fall.

Section 3. All officers and directors who are members in good standing shall be eligible for re-election.

ARTICLE VIII: Meetings

Section 1. The club shall hold regular weekly meetings at such time and place as shall be determined by the club with the approval of the principal.

ARTICLE IX: Committees

Section 1. There should be at least the following standing committees:

a) Kiwanis Family Relations Committee
b) Program Committee
c) Project Committee
d) Public Relations Committee
e) Social Committee
f) Membership Development Committee
g) Major Emphasis Committee

Section 2. The duties of the standing committees shall be as follows:

a)   The Kiwanis Family Relations Committee shall work with the Program and Project Committees in preparing inter-club activities with Kiwanis and Circle K (if one exists in the area) and shall see that the membership of the Key Club and its sponsoring Kiwanis Club are cognizant of all areas of each organization thereof.

b)   The Program Committee shall plan and present programs at all regular meetings, club inductions, and inter-clubs with Key Clubs and other service groups in the school and community, unless otherwise directed by the president. The committee shall arrange for a suitable place for club luncheons and see that the space occupied is made orderly after each meeting.

c)   The Project Committee shall formulate worthwhile activities, and upon approval by the principal, shall recommend them to the club. The projects adopted by the club shall be initiated and completed under the direction of the Project Committee with the aid of the club membership.

d)   The Public Relations Committee shall be responsible for informing the public of the Key Club's activities and goals through the use of articles, photographs, the local newspaper, talks with school officials, radio and television.

e)   The Social Committee shall plan the social activities of the club, such as banquets honoring the fathers and mothers of the members, dances, etc., and entertainment for club meetings.

f)   The Membership Development Committee shall devise effective plans to obtain new members on a regular basis to provide the necessary manpower for an effective program of service.

The Major Emphasis Committee shall plan projects and activities promoting and supporting the Key Club Inter- national Theme and Major Emphasis programs during their administrative years.

ARTICLE X: Annual Dues

Section 1. Total amount dues shall be $_____ per member, which is the sum of $_____ for district dues, $_____ for International dues, and $_____ for individual club dues.

ARTICLE XI: Amendments

Section 1. Amendments to these bylaws shall be adopted by two-thirds (2/3) vote of the members present at any regular meeting held one week or more after a regular meeting at which the proposed amendment or amendments were read, or after giving written notice thereof to each member one week prior to the action on such amendment or amendments.

Section 2. These bylaws and all amendments or additions thereto shall not become effective until approved by the high school principal, the sponsoring Kiwanis club, and Key Club International.

These Bylaws were adopted and approved on
_____, 20_____

(Principal's signature)

_____

(Principal's name printed)

_____

(Kiwanis Club President's signature)

_____

(President's name printed)

_____

CHAPTER TEN

Parliamentary Procedure Practice Demonstration

Purpose

The purpose of the parliamentary procedure practice demonstration is to allow a team of students/participants to create and demonstrate a practice meeting using parliamentary procedure skills. The best way to learn parliamentary procedure and meeting management is to use them in an actual meeting.

Instructions for Parliamentary Procedure Demonstration

1. Divide the group into teams of six. Smaller teams can be used if necessary.

2. Each team should select a chairperson and a secretary.

3. Each team should develop a parli-pro demonstration and conduct two items of business from the agenda on the following page.

4. The secretary should take minutes of the demonstration proceedings and participate in the demonstration.

5. The secretary will be given five minutes at the end of the demonstration to write the minutes. The minutes will be read to the class/ group.

Required Motions

Each team must use the following motions in its demonstration:

Main motion
Amendment
Refer to a committee
Point of order
Division of the house (assembly)
Fix time to which to adjourn
Postpone Definitely

There are eight items of new business on the agenda. To earn full credit, each team must complete the business of two items of their choice. Teams may also create their own business if desired. Some of the required motions may require the teams to create business in order to execute the motions.

Each item must be voted on for credit.

Opening and closing ceremonies are not necessary. The demonstrating team should assume that a regular meeting is in progress. The chairperson should start the demonstration by saying:

"Is there any further business that should be presented at this time?"

Next, a team member should be recognized by the chair and a main motion should be made.

At the end of the meeting the demonstration should be adjourned by a majority vote.

Each team will be given one hour to prepare its demonstration.

The order of team demonstrations will be drawn by the instructor/ facilitator..

Each team demonstration should be completed within ten minutes.

Members should critique each demonstration as they are completed.

AGENDA

Choose a location for the company picnic.

Decide on a fund raiser for the new year.

Should the department purchase awards for outstanding members or employees this year? If so, how should we finance the cost?

How many employees should be sent to the National trade show this year?

What kind of charity program shall our department have this year?

Decide on a new public relations theme for the new year.

What kind of computers should we purchase for the new office?

A local school has asked for a donation. Should we make the donation and if so, how much should it be?

Parliamentary Procedure Demonstration
Score Sheet

Date_____

Teams Members

_____

_____

Items	Points Possible	Score
Main motion	5	_____
Amendment	5	_____
Refer to a committee	5	_____
Point of order	5	_____
Division of the house (assembly)	5	_____
Fix time to which to adjourn	5	_____
Postpone Definitely	5	_____
Business Completed	15	_____
Total Points	50	_____

Comments:

_____

_____

_____

_____

APPENDIX A

Which Motion to use for a Specific Task (Chart)

Which Motion to Use for a Specific Task

TASK	MOTION	PAGE
Bring up an idea or item of business	Main Motion	32
Kill the current motion	Postpone Indefinitely	40
Change or modify a motion	Amend	42
Set up a committee to deal with the current main motion	Refer to a Committee	45
Postpone a motion to a future date	Postpone Definitely	47
Control the debate on a motion: - time per speaker - number of speeches per speaker - time to close debate	Limit or Extend Limits of Debate	49
Request a vote on a pending motion	Previous Question	51
Set a motion aside temporarily	Lay on the Table	53
Demand that the agenda be followed	Call for the Orders of the Day	59
Make a special request	Question of Privilege	61
Request a short break in a meeting	Recess	63
Close a meeting	Adjourn	65
Set the time and place for a future meeting	Fix the Time to Which to Adjourn	66
You think the rules have been broken	Point of Order	72
Disagree with a ruling by the chair	Appeal	74
Request to do something that does not comply with the normal rules of the group	Suspend the Rules	76

TASK	MOTION	PAGE
You don't want a motion to be dealt with	Objection to the Consideration of the Question	77
Separate a motion into distinct parts	Division of a Question	79
You believe a voice vote result was	Division of the House	81
You have a question about parliamentary procedure	Parliamentary Inquiry	83
Ask for information related to the current business	Point of Information	84
Withdraw or change a motion - before it is stated by the chair	Withdraw or Modify a Motion	85
Bring a tabled motion back for further discussion	Take from the Table	94
Get rid of a motion that was passed at a previous meeting	Rescind	96
Bring a motion that was dealt with at a previous meeting back for further discussion	Reconsider	98

APPENDIX B
Motion Details (Chart)

Motion Details Chart (Alphabetized)

MOTION	Must Be Recognized By Chair	In Order When Another Has the Floor	Second	Debate	Amend	Vote	Rec
Adjourn	Yes	No	Yes	No	No	Maj.	No
Amend	Yes	No	Yes	Yes	Yes	Maj.	Yes
Appeal	No	Yes	Yes	Yes	Yes	Maj.	Yes
Call for the orders of the Day	No	Yes	No	No	No	2/3	No
Division of the Assembly	No	Yes	No	No	No	Rise	No
Division of a Question	Yes	No	Yes	No	Yes	Maj.	No
Fix the Time to Which to Adjourn	Yes	No	Yes	No	Yes	Maj.	Yes
Lay on the Table	Yes	No	Yes	No	No	Maj.	No
Limit Debate	Yes	No	Yes	No	Yes	2/3	Yes
Main Motion	Yes	No	Yes	Yes	Yes	Maj.	Yes
Objection to the Consideration of a Question	No	Yes	No	No	No	2/3	Yes
Parliamentary Inquiry	No	Yes	No	No	No	No	No
Point of Information	No	Yes	No	No	No	No	No

Must Be Recognized By Chair - Before a member can speak, he or she must get recognized by the chairperson.

In Order When Another Has the Floor - Depending on the motion on the floor, a member may or may not interrupt the current speaker.

Second - Depending on the motion presented, a second may or may not be required.

Debate - Depending on the motion, members may or may not be allowed to debate.

Amend - Some motions can be amended and some may not.

Vote - Different motions require different types of voting. Majority, two-thirds, etc.

Rec (Reconsider) - Some motions may be reconsidered by the group, others may not.

Motion Details Chart (Alphabetized)

MOTION	Must Be Recognized By Chair	In Order When Another Has the Floor	Second	Debate	Amend	Vote	Rec
Point of Order	No	Yes	No	No	No	No	No
Postpone Definitely	Yes	No	Yes	Yes	Yes	Maj.	Yes
Postpone Indefinitely	Yes	No	Yes	Yes	No	Maj.	Yes
Previous Question	Yes	No	Yes	No	No	2/3	No
Question of Privilege	No	Yes	No	No	No	No	No
Recess	Yes	No	Yes	No	Yes	Maj.	No
Reconsider	Yes	No	Yes	Yes$_1$	No	Maj.	No
Refer to a Committee	Yes	No	Yes	Yes	Yes	Maj.	Yes
Rescind	Yes	No	Yes	Yes	Yes	2	Yes$_3$
Suspend the Rules	Yes	No	Yes	No	No	2/3	No
Take from the Table	Yes	No	Yes	No	No	Maj.	No
Withdraw a Motion	No	Yes	No	No	No	No	No

1 - A motion to reconsider is debatable if the motion proposed to be reconsidered is debatable.

2 - Majority vote with previous notice, or majority of the entire membership without previous notice, or 2/3 vote without previous notice. See page 96.

3 - Can be reconsidered only when the motion to rescind another motion received a negative vote.

APPENDIX C

Correct form for Presenting Motions

Correct form for Presenting Motions

MOTION	CORRECT FORM/EXAMPLE MOTIONS
Adjourn	*I move to adjourn.*
Amend	*I move to amend the main motion by adding...*
Appeal	*I appeal from the decision of the chair.*
Call for the Orders of the Day	*Mr. Chairman, I call for the orders of the day.*
Division of the Assembly	*Division of the house. or Division.*
Division of a Question	*I move to divide the question (or motion) such that the awards banquet and fundraiser are considered separately.*
Fix the Time to Which to Adjourn	*Mr. Chairman, I move that when this meeting adjourns, it stand adjourned to meet Tuesday, March 12, at 7:00PM at the department meeting room.*
Lay on the Table	*I move to lay the motion on the table.*
Limit Debate	*I move to limit debate on the pending motion to five minutes per speaker.*
Main Motion	*I move that the department host an awards banquet in April.*
Objection to the Consideration of a Question	*I object to the consideration of the question.*
Parliamentary Inquiry	*Madam President, I rise to a parliamentary inquiry*
Point of Information	*Mr. Chairman, I rise to a point of information."*

Question - See page 33.

Correct form for Presenting Motions

MOTION	CORRECT FORM/EXAMPLE MOTIONS
Point of Order	*I rise to a point of order. or Point of order.*
Postpone Definitely	*I move to postpone the motion to have an awards banquet until the January meeting.*
Postpone Indefinitely	*I move that the motion to have an awards banquet be postponed indefinitely.*
Previous Question	*I move the previous question.*
Question of Privilege	*Madam President, I rise to a question of personal privilege.*
Recess	*Mr. Chairman, I move to take a five minute recess.*
Reconsider	*I move to reconsider the motion to hold our annual awards banquet in May voted on at the March meeting. I voted for (or against) this motion.*
Refer to a Committee	*I move to refer the motion to a committee of four, with Sue Jones as the chairperson, the members to be appointed by the chair, with the power to act, and to report back at the April meeting.*
Rescind	*I move to rescind the previously adopted main motion concerning the landscaping of the office grounds."*
Suspend the Rules	*I move to suspend the standing rule requiring managers to wear ties at meetings.*
Take from the Table	*I move to take from the table the motion to have a fund raiser which was tabled at our last meeting.*
Withdraw a Motion	*Mr. President, I withdraw the motion*

GLOSSARY

ACCOMPANY
To go along with someone else or to go with something else.

ADDITION
In parliamentary procedure addition refers to adding words or paragraphs to a main motion by making an amendment.

ADJOURN
To close a meeting.

ADOPT
To accept an idea or to choose and follow a course of action.

AFFIRMATIVE
To agree with someone or something.

AGENDA
An agenda is an order of business adopted for a specific meeting or session.

AMEND
To modify or change a motion by adding something to it or subtracting something from it.

AMENDMENT TO THE FIRST DEGREE
The first amendment made to a pending motion. Must be germane to the pending motion.

AMENDMENT TO THE SECOND DEGREE
An amendment to the pending primary amendment. Must be germane to the primary amendment. Also called an amendment to the amendment.

APPEAL
This motion gives a member a device to use when disagreeing with a ruling by the chair.

APPROVAL OF MINUTES
The minutes of the previous meeting should be read by the secretary and approved immediately after the opening of the current meeting.

ASSEMBLY
The group of members at a meeting.

AYE
Pronounced "I". The word used to vote in favor of a motion or course of action; means yes.

BUSINESS AT HAND
The current business being dealt with in a meeting.

BYLAWS
The bylaws of an organization are the rules that govern the functions of the organization.

CALL FOR A MEETING
Notification of the members about an upcoming meeting. Can be accomplished by text, email, letter, phone call, etc.

CALL FOR THE ORDERS OF THE DAY
Motion by which a member can require the assembly to conform to its agenda, program, or order of business.

CHAIR
The officer or person in charge of conducting a meeting.

CHAIRMAN
The officer or person in charge of conducting a meeting.

CHAIRPERSON
The officer or person in charge of conducting a meeting.

CHAIRWOMAN
The officer or person in charge of conducting a meeting.

COMMIT
To refer a motion to a committee.

COMMITTEE
A small group of people within an organization who have a specific task or project to complete.

CONSIDERATION
To discuss and decide on a motion or an item of business in a meeting. To give the motion consideration.

CONSTITUTION
A system of laws and principles used to govern a state or organization.

DEBATE
A formal discussion on a particular topic in which opposing arguments are put forward.

DELEGATE
To give someone a task or job to be completed.

DEMOCRACY
A form of government in which the common people hold political power and can rule either directly or through elected representatives.

DEMOCRATIC
A system that treats everyone equally.

DISCUSSION
Talking or debating about something, especially in order to solve a problem or resolve a question.

DIVISION
Shortened version of the motion "division of the house."

DIVISION OF A QUESTION
When a motion relating to a single subject contains several parts, the parts can be separated to be discussed and voted on as distinct motions.

DIVISION OF THE ASSEMBLY (HOUSE)
If a member believes that a voice or hand vote was not accurate a division of the house motion may be called for. This motion requires the chair to call for a rising vote where members stand and are counted.

FAIL A MOTION
A majority of the members vote negatively on a motion.

FIX THE TIME TO WHICH TO ADJOURN
The purpose of this motion is to set the time, and sometimes the place, for another meeting to continue the business of the current session.

FLOOR
To have the "floor" is to have been recognized by the chairperson and have the right to speak before the assembly or group.

GENERAL CONSENT
In cases where a majority seems obvious the chair can use general consent. An actual motion is not necessary is this case. For example, in the case of approving the minutes the chair would state, "If there is no objection the minutes stand approved as read."

GAVEL

The chairperson uses a gavel (wooden mallet) to keep the meeting on track and to signal the passage or failure of any motions that are proposed by members of the group.

GERMANE

To be relevant and to relate to the pending motion or to the business at hand.

HAND VOTE

Voting by raising hands.

HOUSE

Another word used for assembly or all the members at a meeting.

IN ORDER

A proper motion or action taken at a meeting. The chair decides if a motion is in order or not.

INCIDENTAL MOTIONS

An incidental motion is a motion that relates to the main motion and other parliamentary motions. They take precedence (priority) over any pending question (motion) out of which they arise. Incidental Definition: Happening as a result of or in connection with something more important.

INSERTION

In parliamentary procedure insertion refers to the insertion (putting in) of a word, words, or paragraphs into another motion by making an amendment.

LAY ON THE TABLE

This motion enables the assembly to lay a pending motion aside temporarily when something more urgent has arisen.

LIMIT DEBATE

This motion is used to control debate on a pending motion.

MAIN MOTION

The main motion is used to bring an item of business, an idea, or a proposal before the group.

MAJORITY

One more than half.

MAKER OF THE MOTION

A person who makes a motion during a meeting. The maker of a motion has the first right to discuss the motion.

MINUTES

Official record of the events at a meeting. May include motions passed, presentations, committee reports, new business, etc.

MINUTES OF THE PREVIOUS MEETING

Record of motions and business transacted from a previous meeting.

MODIFY

To make a change or alteration to a motion by making an amendment.

MOTION

A motion is simply a formal way of saying what you want to happen in a meeting.

MOTIONS THAT BRING A QUESTION AGAIN BEFORE THE ASSEMBLY

Motions that bring other motions back from previous meetings for further discussion.

MOVE

To propose a motion or other course of action during a meeting.

NEGATIVE

To be against a motion or other course of action during a meeting.

NEW BUSINESS

New items that need to be brought up and discussed during a meeting.

NO

Word used to vote against a motion.

NOMINATIONS

The individuals who are selected by the members to run for officer or other positions within an organization.

OJECTIVES

Goals or something to aim for.

OBJECTION TO THE CONSIDERATION OF A QUESTION

This motion is used to enable the assembly to avoid a particular main motion; to disagree with or "object" to a motion. It enables a member to propose that a certain motion <u>not</u> be considered.

OBTAIN THE FLOOR

When a member is recognized by the chair they are said to have obtained the floor and have the right to speak.

ORDER OF BUSINESS

A standard order of items to deal with in a meeting. Normally listed on an agenda.

ORGANIZATION

A body (group) of persons organized for some specific purpose, as a club, union, or society.

OUT OF ORDER

When a person incorrectly proposes a motion or proposes the wrong motion they are said to be out of order. The chair determines when a member is out of order. Formally, the chair strikes the gavel one time and declares "out of order."

PARLIAMENTARIAN

A person who is an expert in parliamentary procedures, rules, or debate.

PARLIAMENTARY INQUIRY

A parliamentary inquiry is a question directed to the presiding officer to obtain information on a matter of parliamentary law pertaining to the business at hand.

PARLIAMENTARY LAW

Parliamentary law is the collection of laws, rules and procedures that organizations use to conduct business.

PASS A MOTION

To approve a motion proposed by a member by voting.

PENDING

The current motion or business before the assembly.

PENDING MOTION

The current motion before the assembly.

POINT OF INFORMATION

A request directed to the chair for information relevant to the business at hand, but not related to parliamentary procedure.

POINT OF ORDER

This motion can be used when a member thinks the rules of the assembly have been violated.

POSTPONE DEFINITELY

This motion is used to postpone action on a pending motion to a definite day, time, meeting, or event in the future.

POSTPONE INDEFINITELY

This motion kills the main motion for the duration of the current meeting.

POWER TO ACT

When a member or committee has the authority to conduct business on behalf of the organization.

PRECEDING

Coming before or being ahead of.

PRESIDING OFFICER

The officer in charge of a meeting. Normally the president.

PREVAILING

To be on the winning side of a vote.

PREVIOUS NOTICE

Informing the members of an organization about an upcoming meeting or event. Previous notice is usually given by the chairperson by text, email, etc.

PREVIOUS QUESTION

The previous question is a motion used to bring the assembly to an immediate vote on one or more pending motions. It immediately closes all debate and stops any further amendments.

PRIMARY AMENDMENT
The first amendment made to another pending motion. Must be germane to the pending motion.

PRIVILEGED MOTIONS
Motions which do not relate to the pending question (motion) but have to do with matters of such urgency or importance that, without debate, are allowed to interrupt the consideration of anything else.

PROCEDURE
Order of the steps to be taken to make something happen, or how something is done.

QUESTION
The "question" refers to the formal statement by the chair of the motion presented by a member of the group. As in, "are you ready for the question?" Are you ready to vote on the pending motion?

QUESTION OF PRIVILEGE
This motion permits a member to make a special request at a meeting.

QUORUM
The minimum number of people needed at a meeting to conduct business.

RATIFY
To give formal approval for some action or procedure.

RECESS
A short intermission during a meeting.

RECOGNIZED
To be given the right to speak by the chairperson. You must be Recognized before you can speak, except in certain situations. To be recognized you should stand and address the chair. Madam Chairperson, Mr. Chairperson or Mr. Chairman.

RECONSIDER
A call for a motion to reconsider allows a motion which has already been voted on to be brought back for further consideration.

REFER TO A COMMITTEE
This motion is used to send a pending motion to a small group or committee so that the motion can be carefully investigated and brought back at a later meeting to be considered by the members.

RELEVANT
Connected or related to the current situation.

RESCIND
The motion to rescind is used to strike out an entire main motion, resolution, rule, by-law, section, or paragraph, which was adopted at a previous meeting.

RIGHTS OF THE MINORITY
Each member in an organization must have the right to speak and express their opinion regardless of whether or not their opinion differs from everyone else's.

RISING VOTE
Standing for a vote so a count can be taken. Raising hands is often used as a rising vote.

ROLL CALL
In a roll call vote the secretary polls (asks each member) the group and records how each member votes.

RULE OF THE MAJORITY
When items of business are voted on, the resulting decision will be based on the will of the majority. In other words, the group will do what the majority of members decide.

RULES OF ORDER

Written rules of parliamentary procedure formally adopted by an organization. These rules allow for the orderly transaction of business during meetings.

RULING BY THE CHAIR

Decisions made by the chairperson.

SECOND

To announce "second" once a motion is made in a meeting, is to indicate that you also support bringing the motion before the assembly for discussion. Motion must receive a second in order to be discussed, or it dies.

SECONDARY AMENDMENT

An amendment to a pending primary amendment. Can also be called an amendment to the amendment. Must be germane to the primary amendment. In other words, a proposed change to a primary amendment.

SECRET BALLOT

A secret ballot is a written vote, it is used to maintain the secrecy of each member's vote.

SPECIAL COMMITTEE

Also known as a select or ad hoc committee. A special committee is appointed as the need arises to carry out a specific task. Once the task is completed the committee is dissolved.

SPECIAL RULES

A special rule of order is a parliamentary procedure term for a rule adopted by the organization that relates to procedure or to the duties of officers within meetings.

STANDING COMMITTEES
Standing committees exist permanently. Each standing committee should have a permanent name. For example, Community Relations Committee.

STANDING RULES
Rules related to the management of the organization rather than rules of parliamentary procedure. An example standing rule would be that all meetings begin at 7:00P.M.

STRIKE OUT
To eliminate a specific word or paragraph in a motion.

SUBSIDIARY MOTIONS
A subsidiary motion is a type of motion by which a group deals directly with a main motion prior to, or instead of, voting on the main motion itself. Subsidiary Definition: Something that is secondary in importance.

SUBSTITUTION
To strike out an replace an entire paragraph of a motion by making an amendment.

SUSPEND
To set aside for a specific purpose.

SUSPEND THE RULES
This motion is used when the assembly wishes to do something that violates one or more of its regular rules.

SUSTAIN
To agree with and thereby support a decision made by the chairperson.

SUSTAINED
Agreed to or upheld by the members. For example, a ruling of the chair is sustained.

TAKE FROM TABLE
This motion is used to bring a previously tabled motion back for consideration by the assembly.

TRANSACT
To do, carry on, or conduct business.

TWO-THRIDS VOTE
A two-thirds vote requires that two-thirds of the members must vote in favor of a motion for it to pass.

UNAMIMOUS CONSENT
In cases where a majority seems obvious the chair can use unanimous consent. An actual motion is not necessary is this case. For example, in the case of approving the minutes the chair would state, "If there is no objection the minutes stand approved as read."

UNFINISHED BUSINESS
Business carried over from a previous meeting that still needs to be dealt with in the current meeting.

VIOLATES
To fail to comply with a requirement or rule, to fail to respect someone's privacy or to fail to respect someone or something sacred.

VOICE VOTE
Voting by saying "aye" (yes) or "no."

VOTE
An expression of a choice or a decision by an individual.

WITHDRAW A MOTION

Before a motion has been stated by the chair, it is the property of the person who made it. The maker of a motion can withdraw it or modify it without the consent of anyone.

YIELD

To produce or give something to another, as in "yield the floor." To give back the floor after speaking to a group.

YIELD THE FLOOR

When a member finishes speaking, he or she "yields the floor," or gives the floor back to the chairperson, by resuming his or her seat.

References

Armbruster, Jim. Teacher Services Specialist. National FFA Organization, Indianapolis, IN.

Bredstrand, John. Agriculture Teacher. Evergreen School District, Vancouver, WA.

Clabough, Debbie. Associated Student Body Secretary. Battle Ground Public Schools, Battle Ground, WA.

Hadaller, Kurt. Agriculture Teacher. South Kitsap School District, Port Orchard, WA.

Hunter, Sharon. Developing Leadership and Personal Skills. Illinois: Interstate Publishers, Inc., 1997.

Parliamentary Procedure Made Easy, video. The Parliamentary Procedure Instructional Materials Center.

Ricketts, Cliff. Leadership, Personal Development & Career Success. Delmar Publishers, 1997.

Robert, Henry M. Robert's Rules of Order Newly Revised (1990 Edition) Scott Foresman Publishing, 1990.

Robert, Henry M. Robert's Rules of Order. Boston: De Capo Press, 2011.

Slaughter, James H. Certified Professional Parliamentarian, Greensboro, NC.

About the Author

Christopher G. Yorke graduated from Washington State University in Pullman, Washington. He earned a Bachelor of Arts Degree in Economics and a Bachelor of Science Degree in Agriculture Education. He also earned a Masters Degree in Technical Education from City University in Seattle, Washington.

Mr. Yorke taught Agribusiness, Agriscience, Parliamentary Procedure, and Leadership Skills for 32 years in Washington State. He has conducted numerous parliamentary procedure workshops for ASB groups, classes, and adult organizations. He also trained many parliamentary procedure teams for competition at the State level.

In the private sector Mr. Yorke worked in management positions for Frito-Lay, Inc., J.R. Simplot, Inc., and Acro Publishing, Inc. In these positions leadership and effective meeting skills were utilized on a daily basis. A working knowledge of parliamentary procedure was a definite asset.